MACS EDUARDS

VISUAL ENDTIME STUDY GUIDE

DANIEL & END OF DAYS BIBLE PROPHECY

WestBow Press books may be ordered through booksellers or by contacting:

WestBow Press
A Division of Thomas Nelson & Zondervan
1663 Liberty Drive
Bloomington, IN 47403
www.westbowpress.com
1 (866) 928-1240

Scripture taken from the King James Version of the Bible.

Scripture taken from the New King James Version®. Copyright © 1982 by Thomas Nelson. Used by permission. All rights reserved.

ISBN: 978-1-9736-1649-8 (sc)
ISBN: 978-1-9736-1650-4 (e)

Library of Congress Control Number: 2018908323

Print information available on the last page.

WestBow Press rev. date: 12/03/2019

WESTBOW
P R E S S®
A DIVISION OF THOMAS NELSON
& ZONDERVAN

VISUAL
ENDTIME
STUDY
GUIDE

CONTENTS

INTRODUCTION vii

QUESTION SECTION

ONE WEEK COVENANT... 1

♦ The 7 years will begin with the "wall" of deception and end with the "flood" returning to the pit

LAST DAYS TIMELINE 2

♦ After the falling away, believers and the restrainer are "taken" and the anti-Christ will be revealed

OLIVET DISCOURSE.. 3

♦ Rebuilding the "fallen temple" will bring about the Day of His Coming followed by the End of the Ages

SIGNS OF HIS COMING... 4

♦ In the days of "pre-tribulation" and before angels gather the elect, false prophets will deceive Israel

SIGNS OF THE END 5

♦ After persecution of the saints is shortened, the Gospel will be preached and the abomination is set up

DAY OF HIS COMING 6

♦ The Lord's glory in the heavens, will leave the earth in "darkness" and distress the nations

DAY OF THE LORD 7

♦ Great persecution, followed by quakes and heavenly signs, ending with the "siege" of Jerusalem

7-YEAR TIMELINE... 8

♦ The temple will be cleansed, sacrifices will end and after the siege, the remnant will be blessed

KINGDOMS OF ISRAEL 9

♦ The Northern & Southern kingdoms of Israel, Little horn enters Judah, Jerusalem under siege

ISRAEL'S "CAPTIVITY"...10

♦ God calls peace, no peace! Judah's captivity returns, sin is remembered & Jerusalem is surrounded

JACOB'S TROUBLE 11

♦ Israel, now called "Jacob", is refined in fire for the shedding of blood and their power is scattered

CONTENTS

FIVE OF 7 CHURCHES 12

  * While the "wise" believe and seek Jesus, the "foolish" deny Him and heed the doctrine of false sacrifice

TWO OF 7 CHURCHES 13

  * Philadelphia is kept from trial, while Laodicea is tested for failing to heed the 7 Spirits of God

FALSE PROPHET 14

  * The False Prophet deceives and leads the world to worship the Beast and to receive his mark

ANTI-CHRIST 15

  * Anti-Christ is given power to overcome the world, while Israel first receives him, then resists him

SALVATION OF GOD 16

  * God has provided Jesus as His salvation to the Gentiles after first visiting Israel, His "chosen"

SALVATION IS REJECTED 17

  * Limiting Jesus as God's offering for sin, rejects His salvation and limits the Holy One of Israel

7 SEALS ARE OPENED 18

  * On the "Day of the Lord" a 4th of the earth is slain, stars fall to the earth and Heaven is silent

7 TRUMPETS 19

  * Falling star "Wormwood" kills a third of men, the bittersweet book is eaten, the end is a "flood"

7 ANGELS OF THE HARVEST 20

  * The Everlasting Gospel is preached, Babylon falls and men with the mark of the Beast are tormented

7 PLAGUES 21

  * None can enter when God's glory fills the temple, God remembers Babylon and the blood of His saints

JUDGMENTS 22

  * Graph of the 7 Seals, 7 Trumpets, 7 Plagues and the Harvest

ANSWER SECTION

ANSWER SECTION & MAIN GRAPHS 23

TEST YOUR KNOWLEDGE

1. When will the (*temple*) "wall" be built? ... ... (Pre) (Mid-week) (Post) ... ... Page 1

2. How will the end be with a "flood"? ... ... Page 1

3. Who "devises" the covenant that anti-Christ confirms? ... ... Page 1

4. What is the "falling away" that comes first? ... ... Page 2

5. Who restrains the "lawlessness" of Satan? ... ... Page 2

6. How will prophets deceive Israel? ... ... Page 4

7. When will be the Day of His coming? ... ... (Pre) (Mid-week) (Post) ... ... Page 4

8. When will Angels gather the elect? ... ... (Pre) (Mid-week) (Post) ... ... Page 4

9. How will days of "persecution" be shortened? ... ... Page 5

10. How long will be the "Day of Christ"? ... ... Page 6

11. When will armies surround Jerusalem? ... ... (Pre) (Mid-week) (Post) ... ... Page 7

12. When will the "Abomination" be set-up? ... ... (Pre) (Mid-week) (Post) ... ... Page 8

13. Who will have "tribulation 10 days"? ... ... Page 8

14. When will Little horn enter Jerusalem? ... ... (Pre) (Mid-week) (Post) ... ... Page 9

15. Why will Israel "return" to captivity? ... ... Page 10

16. When will the Holy people have power? ... ... (Pre) (Mid-week) (Post) ... ... Page 11

17. When will the church be taken? ... ... (Pre) (Mid-week) (Post) ... ... Page 13

18. When will Little horn war with the saints? ... ... (Pre) (Mid-week) (Post) ... ... Page 15

19. What is the "half-hour of silence" in Heaven? ... ... Page 18

20. Which days will be darkened? ... ... Page 19

21. What is the "Bittersweet Little Book"? ... ... Page 19

22. When will the "Gospel" be preached? ... ... (Pre) (Mid-week) (Post) ... ... Page 20

23. Why did God allow Satan to torment Job? ... ... Page 32

24. Where will "Mystery, Babylon" be found? ... ... Page 21

DEDICATION

~ Israel was recognized as a nation on May 14, 1948 ~
This book is dedicated to the "70 year anniversary" of Israel in their land!

INTRODUCTION

This study guide was created to unveil complex information about the final days. Before my son Bryan was taken to be with the Lord, he shared a deep desire to understand End-time prophecies and as a father I wanted to answer his questions knowledgeably. I began a twelve-year quest to diligently search the Scriptures for answers that have been hidden until now (*Daniel 12:9*).

The secret things belong unto the LORD our God,
But those things which are revealed belong to us and our children forever. Deut 29:29 (KJV)

The purpose of this book is to provide the reader with a visual timeline of the future events that will occur during the 7-year tribulation period. Key prophetic verses, mainly from the books of Daniel, Revelation and the Prophets, are combined into one cohesive Study Guide. At the end of this study, the reader should have a good understanding of the various signs of the End-times and the order that events will occur.

HOW TO USE THIS STUDY GUIDE

Each page of the book covers a specific topic of interest such as the 7 Year Covenant of Daniel, Salvation of God, Anti-Christ, Mystery Babylon or the Day of His Coming. Mini graphs high-light key points and place prophetic events in chronological order. These mini graphs merge into one main graph located at the end of the book. This all- encompassing timeline can be more fully appreciated once the Study Guide and Answer Section are completed. To help with visualization, the color graphs have various tones of Red to represent EVIL Blue for GOOD and Purple for JUDGMENT .

QUESTION AND ANSWER SECTIONS

This booklet is divided into 2 sections. The first section of the book introduces 24 questions which are derived from familiar End-time prophecy verses such as "What is the falling away?", "When will the church be taken?" or "What is the bitter-sweet little book?" The answers can be found in the second section of the book, along with an overview of the material. All information given comes from key Bible verses and the author's brief commentaries indicated by this symbol (❖) are based on conclusions that those passages reveal. The intent of the booklet is to guide the reader, but allow the Scripture verses to speak for themselves.

Search the Scriptures!

INTRODUCTION

THE GUIDE AS A COMPANION TO THE BIBLE

Your own Bible is recommended as a companion to this booklet for complete verse and context. The Old King James (KJV) is preferred over other versions because it provides a correct study of End-time Prophecy. The New International Version (NIV) for example, uses words such as "*fortune*" or "*exile*" in place of "*captivity*". This Guide will show how the captivity of Israel will be possible even while they are living safely in their land. It is quite different from the Babylonian captivity, which was in a foreign land! After nearly 2,000 years of exile, Israel was again recognized as a nation in 1948. However, there will be a future time when Israel will backslide and go into self- imposed bondage while living in their land! It should also be noted that the chronology of prophecy does not usually follow the same order as does the written text. For example, in II Thessalonians 2:3-7, the Day of Christ is stated first, but it is the final event! Wherever the Old King James Version is used, expressions such as thee and thou, or couldest may be modernized.

THE SEVENTY WEEKS OF DANIEL

The biblical account of the prophet Daniel began approximately around 604 BC when he, along with other Jewish young men, was taken captive by the Babylonian king Nebuchadnezzar. After nearly 70 years of captivity, Daniel prayed to God for mercy on behalf of his people. The angel Gabriel revealed to Daniel a series of future prophetic events known as the Seventy Weeks of Daniel. It is important to understand that the Hebrew word *weeks* or *sevens* literally means a week of years. Therefore, in this passage of the Bible, one week equals 7 years and 70 weeks equal 490 years. The final 7 years in this prophecy (*Daniel 9:27*) is commonly known as the 70th Week of Daniel or the One Week Covenant of Daniel.

ARE WE IN THE FINAL DAYS?

This is a serious question that many of us are asking today, in light of all that is going on in the world around us. Although the Bible does not specifically tell us the exact date, it does give us many clues as to what signs to expect that herald the End-Days. Some information remains a mystery, however God has revealed many details to the believers so that we are prepared and not caught off guard when that day comes. Even though this is a sobering subject, we have the hope of eternal life and God's promise that we are not appointed to suffer through the time of wrath.

> *For God did not appoint us to wrath, but to obtain salvation through our Lord Jesus Christ, who died for us, that whether we wake or sleep, we should live together with Him* ~ **I Thes 5:9-10 (NKJ)**

So, what should we do with this knowledge? Knowing about the future coming of the Lord is foolish wisdom if we delay or die before we accept Jesus as our Lord and Savior. So, we should search the scriptures for our own answers, begin a personal relationship with God and share the knowledge with others. The word of God is the most powerful weapon in your spiritual arsenal, so share with others the good news of the Gospel of Salvation!

> *For God so loved the world that He gave His only begotten Son, that whoever believes in Him should not perish but have eternal life* ~ **John 3:16 (NKJ)**

INTRODUCTION

THE 70 WEEKS OF DANIEL

> **One week = 7 years**

Fulfill her <u>week</u>, and we will give thee this (Rachel) also for the service which thou (Jacob) shalt serve me yet 7 other <u>years</u>. **Genesis 29:27** (KJV)

> **70 weeks x 7 years = 490 years**

God deals with sin for eternity:
Daniel 9:24 ~ 70 weeks (*490 years*) are determined upon thy people and upon Thy Holy city, to finish the transgression, and to make an end of sins, and to make reconciliation for iniquity (sin), and to bring in everlasting righteousness, and to seal up the vision and prophecy, and to anoint the Most Holy. (KJV)

❖ *In a future time, the Lord will put an end to sin and bring everlasting righteousness!* ❖

> **69 weeks x 7 years = 483 years**

Jerusalem is restored:
Dan 9:25 ~ Know therefore and understand, that from the going forth of the commandment to restore and to build Jerusalem until Messiah the Prince (*Christ*) there shall be 7 weeks, and 62 weeks (*483 years*); the street shall be built again, and the "wall", even in troublous (*troublesome*) times. (KJV)

❖ *Daniel's vison of a future wall being built in troubled times, has a physical & a spiritual meaning!* ❖

The crucifixion of Jesus:
Dan 9:26 ~ And after the 62 weeks shall Messiah be cut off, but not for Himself; and the people of the prince that shall come (*Anti-Christ*) shall destroy the city and the sanctuary; and the end thereof shall be with a flood, and unto the end of the war desolations are determined. (KJV)

❖ *This prophecy refers to the crucifixion of Jesus and the future appearance of anti-Christ!* ❖

> **490 – 483 = 7 years**

One Week/7 Year Covenant of Daniel:
Dan 9:27 ~ And he (*Anti-Christ*) shall confirm the covenant with many for one week (*7 years*) and in the midst of the week (*3½ years*) he shall cause the sacrifice and the oblation (*religious offering*) to cease, and for the overspreading of abominations he shall make it desolate, even until the consummation, and that determined shall be poured upon the desolate. (KJV)

❖ *The beginning, middle & end of Daniel 9:27 determine the chronology of the final days!* ❖

ONE WEEK COVENANT

God deals with sin:

Daniel 9:24 70 weeks are determined upon thy people and upon Thy Holy city, to finish the transgression, and to make an end of sins, and to make reconciliation for iniquity, and to bring in everlasting righteousness, and to seal up the vision and prophecy, and to anoint the Most-Holy. (KJV)

The "wall" is built:

Dan 9:25 Know therefore and understand, that from the going forth of the commandment to restore and to build Jerusalem unto the Messiah the Prince (*Christ*) shall be 7 weeks, and 62 weeks: the street shall be built again, and the *"wall"*, even in troublous (*troublesome*) times. (KJV)

> 1. When will the "wall" be built? ... (Pre) (Mid-week) (Post) ... Page 26

❖ *The "wall" that they build becomes an "altar to sin" for Israel ~ Hosea 8:11* ❖

❖ *(Pre) = before Mid-week ... ... (Post) = after Mid-week* ❖

The end with a "flood":

Dan 9:26 And after the 62 weeks shall Messiah be cut off, but not for Himself: and the people of the prince that shall come (*Anti-Christ*) shall destroy the city and the sanctuary; and the end thereof shall be with a *"flood"*, and unto the end of the war desolations are determined. (KJV)

The waters shall never again become a "flood" to destroy all flesh. **Gen 9:15** (NKJ)

> 2. How will the end be with a flood? ... Page 34

And the earth opened its mouth and swallowed up the "flood..." **Rev 12:16** (NKJ)

One Week Covenant

Covenant is confirmed:

Dan 9:27 And he (*Anti-Christ*) shall confirm the covenant with many for one week (*7 years*) and in the midst of the week he shall cause the sacrifice and the oblation to cease, and for the overspreading of abominations he shall make it desolate, even until the consummation, and that determined shall be poured upon the desolate. (KJV)

And he was given authority to continue for 42 months... **Rev 13:5** (NKJ)

> 3. Who "devises" the covenant that anti-Christ confirms? ... Page 25

❖ *Anti-Christ is one of many who confirm the covenant, but he is not yet revealed!* ❖

Street is built & the "wall" in troublesome times!	One-week Covenant	
he confirms covenant...	Mid - week	The end with a "flood"
	...he ends sacrifices	...he makes desolate

Search the Scriptures!

Gathering together: (4)

II Thessalonians 2:1 Now we beseech you, brethren, by the coming of our Lord Jesus Christ, and by our gathering together unto him, (KJV)

*He shall send His angels… and they shall gather together His elect…**Mat 24:31** (KJV)*

Day of Christ: (5)

II The 2:2 That ye be not soon shaken in mind, or be troubled, neither by spirit, nor by word, nor by letter as from us, as that the Day of Christ is at hand. (KJV)

*Day of the Lord: As destruction from the Almighty shall it come… **Joel 1:15** (KJV)*

Falling away is first: (1)

II The 2:3 Let no man deceive you by any means: for that Day shall not come, except there comes a falling away first, and that man of sin be revealed, the son of perdition; **4** who opposes and exalts himself above all that is called God, or that is worshipped; so that he as God sits in the temple of God, showing himself that he is God. (KJV)

4. What is the "falling away" that comes first? … Page 27

"Lawlessness" of Satan!

The "restrainer" is taken: (2)

II The 2:5 Remember ye not, that, when I was yet with you, I told you these things? **6** And now ye know what (is) withholding (restraining) that he might be revealed in his time. **7** For the mystery of *iniquity* (lawlessness) doth already work: only he who now *letteth* (restrains) will let (restrain), until he be taken out of the way. (KJV)

5. Who restrains the "lawlessness" of Satan? … Page 31

*Because he (devil) knows that he has a short time. ~**Rev 12:12** (KJV)*

❖ *When the restrainer is taken, the power of Satan is no longer limited* ❖

"Anti-Christ" is revealed: (3)

II The 2:8 And then shall that *"Wicked"* (*Lawless one/anti-Christ*) be revealed, whom the Lord shall consume with the Spirit of His mouth, and shall destroy with the brightness of His coming: **9** Even him, whose coming is after the *working of Satan* with all power and signs and lying wonders, **10** and with all (*deception and*) unrighteousness in them that perish; because they received not the *love of the truth*, that they might be saved. **11** And for this cause, God shall send them *strong delusion*, that they should believe a lie: (KJV)

*If another shall come in his own name, him ye will receive… **John 5:43** (KJV)*

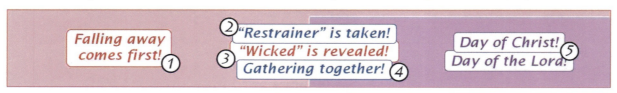

❖ *Mid-week: anti-Christ is revealed when he ends daily sacrifices & Satan is no longer restrained* ❖

OLIVET DISCOURSE

Temple prophecy:

Matthew 24:1 And Jesus went out and departed from the temple: and His disciples came to Him for to show Him the buildings of the temple. **2** And Jesus said unto them, See ye not all these things? Verily I say unto you, there shall not be left here one stone upon another that shall not be thrown down. (KJV)

Temple destruction: 70 A.D.
❖ *The temple was burned & Roman soldiers removed the stones to retrieve melted gold!* ❖

His coming & signs of the end:

Mat 24:3 And as he sat upon the mount of Olives, the disciples came unto him privately, saying, "Tell us, when shall these things be? And what shall be the sign of Thy coming, and of the end of the world?" (KJV)

❖ *Jesus on Mount of Olives* ❖

Signs of His coming: Matthew 24:23-39 ~ Mark 13:21-37 ~ Luke 21:25-36

Column 1 ~ Before His coming:
During the falling away, the street will be built and the *"wall"*! Anti-Christ will confirm the covenant as one of many, but he will not be revealed yet.

Column 2 ~ Day of His coming:
Mid-week angels of the Lord will gather His elect and the *"restrainer"* will be taken away! Anti-Christ will end daily sacrifices and he will be revealed at this time.

Signs of the end: Matthew 24:4-22 ~ Mark 13:5-20 ~ Luke 21:8-24

Column 3 ~ Signs of the End:
The *"Day of Christ"* will begin and the Lord will allow the Anti-Christ to have power for the final 42 months. The end will be with a *"flood"* from the pit, but not a flood of water!

❖ *OLIVET DISCOURSE: The Lord reveals End-time prophecies on the Mount of Olives!* ❖

Be ready for the Coming Wedding!
*Many are soon to be taken and some will not have accepted the Lord! **Mat 22:10-13***

Before His Coming!

False prophets deceive Israel:

Matthew 24:23 Then if any man shall say unto you, lo, here is Christ, or there; believe it not. **24** For there shall arise false Christs, and false prophets, and shall show great signs and wonders; insomuch that, if it were possible, they shall deceive the very elect. **26** Wherefore if they shall say unto you, Behold, he is in the desert; go not forth: behold, he is in the secret chambers; believe it not. **27** For as the lightning cometh out of the east, and shines even unto the west; so, shall also the coming of the Son of man be. (KJV)

*I sent them not, yet they say, "Sword and famine shall not be in this land…" **Jer 14:15** (KJV)*

6. How will prophets deceive Israel? … Page 28

❖ *Because of their unbelief, Israel will be deceived by signs & wonders!* ❖

"Those days" of tribulation:

Mat 24:28 For wheresoever the carcass is, there will the eagles be gathered together. **29** Immediately after the tribulation of those days (*not great tribulation*) shall the sun be darkened, and the moon shall not give her light, and the stars shall fall from heaven, and the powers of the heavens shall be shaken. (KJV)

❖ *Believers are told: "In the world ye shall have tribulation…" John 16:33* ❖

Day of His Coming!

Son of Man in Glory!

Mat 24:30 Then the sign of the *Son of Man* will appear in heaven, and then all the tribes of the earth will *"mourn"*, and they will see the *Son of Man* coming on the clouds of heaven with power and great glory. (KJV)

*Selah. His glory covered the heavens… **Habakkuk 3:3** (KJV)*

7. When will be the "Day of His coming"? … (Pre) (Mid-week) (Post) … Page 29

❖ *His coming: His glory "covers" the heavens, believers are taken & the earth mourns!* ❖

The Elect/Believers!

Angels Gather His Elect:

Mat 24:31 And He shall send His angels with a great sound of a trumpet, and they shall *gather together His elect* from the four winds, from one end of heaven to the other. **36** But of that day and hour knows no man, no, not the angels of Heaven, but My Father only. (KJV)

8. When will Angels gather the elect? ... (Pre) (Mid-week) (Post) … Page 29

❖ *The "gathering together of the elect" is also known as "The Rapture"!* ❖

Before His coming!		Mid-week: His coming!	
False prophets deceive Israel!	Tribulation of those days!	Son of Man in power and glory!	Elect are gathered!

❖ *Non-believers are warned: "For then shall be great tribulation…" Mat 24:21* ❖

SIGNS OF THE END

Sorrows begin: (1,260 days)
Matthew 24:7 For nation shall rise against nation; and kingdom against kingdom: and there shall be famines, and pestilences, and earthquakes, in diverse places. **8** All these are the beginning of sorrows. (KJV)

The Elect/Remnant!

Hated for Jesus' sake:
Mat 24:9 Then shall they deliver you up to be afflicted and shall kill you: and you shall be hated of all nations for my name's sake. **10** And then shall many be offended, and shall betray one another, and shall hate one another. **11** And many false prophets shall rise and shall deceive many. **12** And because iniquity shall abound, the love of many shall wax cold. **13** But he that shall endure unto the end, the same shall be saved. (KJV)

*5th seal: The souls of them that were slain for the Word of God... **Rev 6:9** (KJV)*

❖ **Elect/Remnant: they wait too long to accept Jesus and suffer great tribulation!** ❖

Gospel is preached: (30 days)
Mat 24:14 And this gospel of the kingdom shall be preached in all the world for a witness unto all nations; and then shall the end come. (KJV)

*I will give you pastors according to mine heart, which shall feed you knowledge... **Jer 3:15** (KJV)*

Abomination in Holy place:
Mat 24:15 When ye therefore shall see the abomination of desolation spoken of by Daniel the prophet, stand in the Holy place, **16** Then let them which be in Judea flee into the mountains: **17** Let him which is on the housetop not come down to take anything out of his house: **18** Neither let him which is in the field return-back to take his clothes. **19** And woe unto them that are with child, and to them that give suck in those days! **20** But pray ye that your flight be not in the winter, neither on the Sabbath day. (KJV)

*O children of Benjamin, "Gather yourselves to flee out of the midst of Jerusalem!" **Jer 6:1** (KJV)*

Great Tribulation (1,260 days)!

The days are shortened:
Mat 24:21 For then shall be "great tribulation", such as was not since the beginning of the world to this time, no, nor ever shall be. **22** And except those days should be shortened, there should no flesh be saved: but for the *elect/remnant* sake those *(1,260)* days shall be *"shortened"*. (KJV)

*1,260 days: They (saints) shall be given into his (horn's) hand for 3½ years... **Dan 7:25** (KJV)*

9. How will the days of persecution be shortened? ... Page 32

Beginning of sorrows!	Hated for Jesus' sake!	Signs of the end! Days are shortened!	Gospel is preached!	Abomination in Holy place!

*How long, O Lord, Holy and true, until You judge and avenge our blood? **Rev 6:10** (KJV)*

Signs of His Coming!

Distress of nations:

Luke 21:25 There shall be signs in the sun, in the moon, and in the stars; upon the earth distress of nations, with perplexity, the sea and the waves roaring; **26** Men's hearts failing them for "*fear*", and for looking after the things which are coming on the earth; powers of heaven shall be shaken… (KJV)

I will shake the heavens, and the earth shall remove out of her place… **Isa 13:13** (KJV)
❖ ***Fear of the Lord will come to all men when He shakes the heavens & Earth!***❖

The Son of Man in a Cloud!

Power & great glory:

Luke 21:27 And then shall they see the *Son of Man* coming in a cloud with power and *great glory*. **28** And when these things begin to come to pass, then look up, and lift your heads up; for your redemption draws nigh. (KJV)

Stars of heaven and the constellations thereof shall not give their light ~**Isa 13:10** (KJV)
❖ ***Brightness of His glory will "overwhelm" the sun, moon & heavenly lights!*** ❖

Analogy of the fig tree:

Luke 21:29 And He spoke to them a parable, "Behold the fig tree, and all the trees". **30** When they now shoot forth, you see and know of your own selves that summer is now nigh at hand. **31** So like-wise, when you see these things come to pass, know that the kingdom of God is nigh (*near*) at hand. **32** Verily I say unto you, "This <u>generation</u> shall not pass away, till all be fulfilled". **33** Heaven and earth shall pass away; but My words shall not pass away. (KJV)

The time is fulfilled, and the "kingdom of God" is at hand. ~**Mark 1:15** (KJV)
❖ ***1948: The generation that sees Israel in their land will see God's words fulfilled!*** ❖

Day of the Lord begins!

The Day of Christ as a snare:

Luke 21:34 And take heed to yourselves, lest at any time your hearts be overcharged with surfeiting, and drunkenness, and cares of this life, and so that day (*of Christ*) come upon you unawares. **35** For *as a snare* shall it come on all them that dwell on the face of the whole earth. **36** Watch ye therefore, and pray always, that ye may be accounted worthy to escape all these things that shall come to pass, and to stand before the Son of man. (KJV)

The day of the LORD is darkness, and not light! ~**Amos 5:18** (KJV)

10. How long will be the "Day of the Lord"? … Page 30

❖ ***Day of the Lord: Christ gathers His elect, the seals are opened & judgment begins!*** ❖

Day of His Coming (Mid-week)!			Signs of the End!
Cares of this world!	Son of Man comes in power & glory!	Distress of nations!	Day of the Lord! Day of Christ!

Day of the Lord: Alas! It shall come as destruction from the Almighty… **Joel 1:15** (NKJ)

Signs of the End!

Quakes & heavenly signs:

Luke 21:10 Then He said unto them, "Nation will rise against nation, and kingdom against kingdom." **11** And great earthquakes shall be in diverse places, and famines, and pestilences; and fearful sights and great signs shall there be from heaven. (KJV)

*6th seal: a great earthquake; and the stars of heaven fell… **Rev 6:12-13** (KJV)*

Persecuted for Jesus' sake:

Luke 21:12 *"But before all these"*, they shall lay their hands on you, and persecute you, delivering you up to the synagogues, and into prisons, being brought before kings and rulers for My name's sake. **13** And it shall turn to you for a testimony. **14** Settle it therefore in your hearts, not to meditate before what you shall answer: **15** For I will give you a mouth and wisdom, which all your adversaries shall not be able to gainsay (*contradict*) nor resist. **16** And you shall be betrayed both by parents, and brethren, and kinsfolks, and friends; and some of you shall they cause to be put to death. (*first 4 seals: see Rev 6:1-8*) **17** And ye shall be hated of all men for My Name (*Jesus'*) sake. **19** In your patience possess ye your souls. (KJV)

*5th seal: the souls of them that were slain for the Word of God… **Rev 6:9** (KJV)*

Jerusalem is surrounded!

390-day siege: Desolation is near!

Luke 21:20 And when you shall see *Jerusalem* compassed with armies, then know that the desolation thereof is nigh. **21** Then let them which are in *"Judea"* flee to the mountains; and let them which are in the midst of it depart out; and let not them that are in the countries enter therein. (KJV)

*Come out of (Babylon), My people, that ye be not partakers of her sins… **Rev 18:4** (KJV)*

11. When will armies surround Jerusalem? … (Pre) (Mid-week) (Post) … Page 34

*390 days have I laid upon **thee** (for) the years of their iniquity… **Ezekiel 4:5** (KJV)*

Time of the Gentiles!

42 months (1,260 days):

Luke 21:22 For these are the days of vengeance, that all things which are written may be fulfilled. **23** But woe unto them that are with child, and to them that give suck, in those days! For there shall be great distress in the land, and wrath upon this people. **24** And they shall fall by the sword, and shall be led away captive into all nations; and Jerusalem shall be trodden down of the gentiles, until the time of the gentiles be fulfilled. (KJV)

*And the Holy city shall they/gentiles tread under foot 42 months (1,260 days…) **Rev 11:2** (KJV)*

Day of the Lord!

| 5 seals: those persecuted for Jesus' sake! | 42 months: gentiles trample Jerusalem! | 6th seal: Quakes & heavenly signs! | 390-day siege: armies surround Jerusalem ! |

❖ *Jerusalem will be trampled because Israel "trampled" the blood of Jesus!* ❖

2,520 days

One-week Covenant:
Daniel 9:27 And he shall confirm the covenant with many for one week (*7 years/2,520 days*) …
Isaiah 28:15 We have made a *covenant with death*, and with *hell* are we at agreement… **18** And your covenant with death shall be disannulled, and your agreement with hell shall not stand… (KJV)

2,300 days: for Sanctuary cleansing!
Dan 8:13 Another saint said unto that certain saint which spoke "How long shall be the vision concerning the daily sacrifice, and the transgression of desolation, to give both the sanctuary and the host to be trodden under foot?" **14** And he said unto me, "Unto *2,300 days*; then shall the sanctuary be cleansed." (KJV)

220 days: For Sanctuary pollution!
Dan 11:31 They shall "*pollute*" the sanctuary of strength, and shall take away the daily sacrifice…
Eze 7:22 They shall *pollute* my secret place: for the robbers shall enter-into it and defile it… (KJV)

1,290 days!

End of sacrifice to the Abomination:
Dan 12:11 And from the time that the *daily sacrifice* shall be taken away, and the *abomination* that makes desolate set up, there shall be *1,290 days*. (KJV)

> **12. When will the Abomination be set-up? … (Pre) (Mid-week) (Post) … Page 34**

1,260 days: They are "fed" the Gospel!
Rev 10:2 And he (*Mighty Angel*) had in His hand a "*little book*" open. **10** And I took the *little book* out of the Angel's hand, and "*ate*" it up, and it was in my mouth *sweet* as honey: and as soon as I had eaten it, my belly was *bitter*. **12:6** And the woman (*144,000*) fled into the wilderness, where she hath a place prepared of God, that they should "*feed*" her there *1,260 days*. (KJV)

30 days: To preach the Gospel!
Rev 10:11 And He said unto me, "You (*144,000*) must prophesy again before many peoples, nations, tongues, and kings." **14:6** And I saw another angel fly in the midst of Heaven, having the *Everlasting Gospel* (*Little Book*) to preach (*30 days*) unto them that dwell on the earth, and to every nation, kindred, tongue, and people. (KJV)

This gospel of the kingdom shall be preached in all the world, and then shall the end come… Mat 24:14 (KJV)

❖**1,290 days: The 144,000 are "fed" the Gospel 1,260 days & preach 30 days!** ❖

---

10 days: Time of their testing!
Rev 2:10 Fear none of those things which thou shalt suffer: behold, the devil shall cast some of you into prison, that you may be tried (*tested*); and "*you*" shall have tribulation *10 days*… (KJV)

> **13. Who will have "tribulation 10 days"? … Page 33**

2,520 days ~ 7-year Covenant!			
220 days	2,300 days: time needed to cleanse polluted temple!		
	1,000 days: Duration of daily sacrifice!	1,290 days: end of sacrifice to Abomination!	10
		1,260 days: 144,000 "fed" the Gospel	30

Northern Kingdom: 10 tribes disperse!

I Kings 11:31 Behold, I will rend the kingdom out of the hand of Solomon, & will give *10 tribes* to thee (*Jeroboam*)…
12:31 and (he) made priests of the lowest of the people, which were not of the sons of *Levi*…
II Kings 17:6 The king of Assyria took Samaria (*10 tribes*) away into Assyria… (KJV)

❖ *House of Israel*: *10 tribes of the Northern Kingdom (also called Samaria or Ephraim)!* ❖

Southern Kingdom: 2 tribes remain!

I Kings 12:21 And when *Rehoboam* was come to Jerusalem, he assembled all the house of **Judah**, with the tribe of **Benjamin**, (*180,000*) chosen men who were warriors, to fight against the house of *Israel* (*Jeroboam*)… (KJV)

❖ *House of Judah*: *2 tribes of the Southern kingdom were Judah & Benjamin!* ❖

Northern Kingdom: 10 Tribes return!

Eze 37:21 Thus says the Lord GOD; Behold, I will take the children (*10 tribes*) of *Israel* from among the heathen, where they be gone, and will gather them on every side, and bring them into their own land… (KJV)

❖ *Northern kingdom/10 Tribes*: *Exiles returning to Israel in 1948 fulfills this prophecy!* ❖

> *Reuben~Simeon~Issachar~Zebulun~Dan~Asher~Gad~Naphtali~Ephraim~Manasseh*

❖ *Ephraim & Manasseh* *represent the double portion given to* *Joseph* *by Israel in Gen 48:22!* ❖

JERUSALEM IN THE FINAL DAYS

Little Horn!

Little Horn enters Jerusalem:

Dan 8:9 And out of one of them (*4 notable horns*) came forth a *little horn* (*anti-Christ*), which waxed (*grew*) exceeding great, toward the south, and toward the east, and toward the pleasant land/Jerusalem. **23** A king (*little horn*) of fierce countenance, and understanding dark sentences, shall stand up… **24** And his power shall be mighty, but not by his own power: and he shall destroy wonderfully, and shall prosper, and practice, and shall destroy the mighty and the holy people.

Lam 4:12 The kings of the earth, and all inhabitants of the world, would not have believed that the adversary (*Satan*) and the enemy (*anti-Christ*) should have entered the gates of *Jerusalem*. (KJV)

> **14. When will the little horn enter Jerusalem? … (Pre) (Mid-week) (Post) … Page 31**

390-day siege of Jerusalem:

Eze 4:3 And set thy face against it (*Jerusalem*), and it shall be besieged; and thou shalt lay siege against it. **5** For I have laid upon thee the years of their iniquity, according to the number of the days, *390 days: so shalt thou bear their iniquity.* **5:2** Thou shalt burn with fire a *third part* in the midst of the city, when the days of the siege are fulfilled…
Rev 9:15 And the four angels were loosed, which were prepared for an hour, and a day, and a month (*30 days*), and a year (*360 days*), for to slay the *third part* of men. (KJV)

Kingdoms of Israel		
Northern kingdom: 10 tribes return!	Little horn enters S. Kingdom (Judah)!	390 days: siege of Jerusalem!

Prophets say, "Peace"!

God says, "No Peace"!

Jeremiah 5:31 The prophets prophesy falsely, and the priests bear rule by their means; and My people love to have it so: and what will ye do in the end thereof? **6:14** They (*prophet & priest*) have healed also the hurt of the daughter of my people slightly, saying, Peace, peace; when there is no peace. (KJV)

❖ *Deception by false prophets brings "captivity" back to Israel!* ❖

"Pride" brings captivity:

Jacob rejoices & Israel is glad:

Jer 13:17 But if ye will not hear it, my soul shall weep in secret places for your *"pride"*; and mine eye shall weep sore, and run down with tears, because the Lord's flock is carried away captive. **30:3** For, lo, the days come, says the LORD, that I will bring again the *"captivity"* of my people Israel and Judah, says the LORD. **Isa 9:9** *Ephraim* and the inhabitant of *Samaria (N. Kingdom/Israel)*, that say in the *"pride"* and stoutness of heart: **10** The bricks are fallen (*down*), but *we will build* with hewn stones, the sycamores are cut down, but we will change them into cedars. (KJV) (*The 10 dispersed tribes are often called Ephraim and Samaria*)

❖ *Building the temple in pride displeases God and causes their "captivity"!* ❖

Ps 14:7 When the LORD brings back (*their*) captivity, let Jacob rejoice and Israel be glad…**53:6** Oh that the salvation of Israel were come out of Zion! When God brings back the captivity of his people, Jacob shall rejoice, and Israel shall be glad. (KJV)

15. Why does Israel return to captivity? … Page 28

❖ *Israel/Jacob shall rejoice when the temple is built, and sacrifice begins!* ❖

Jerusalem is forgotten 70 years!

Forgotten "sin" is remembered:

Isa 23:15 And it shall come to pass in that day that *Tyre/Jerusalem* shall be forgotten *70 years*.
Eze 21:24 Ye have made your *iniquity/sin* to be remembered, in that your *transgressions/sins* are discovered…

❖ *The "sins" of Israel are forgotten until they return to "sin" sacrifice!* ❖

390-day siege: Jerusalem is surrounded!

Nations are gathered:

Joel 3:2 I will also gather all nations and will bring them down into the valley of Jehoshaphat and will plead with them there for My people and for My heritage Israel, whom they have scattered among the nations and parted my land. (KJV)

*The great city was divided into 3 parts, & the cities of the nations, fell… **Rev 16:19** (KJV)*

Israel's captivity!			
Israel says, Peace! God says, No peace!	Jacob rejoices! Israel is glad!	Israel's forgotten sin is remembered!	God gathers nations to surround Jerusalem!

❖ *1948-2018: Israel celebrates the return to their land after 70 years!* ❖

JACOB'S TROUBLE

Jacob resisted God!

Jacob is called "Israel":

Genesis 32:28 Thy name shall be called *no more Jacob*, but *Israel*: for as a prince hast thou power with God and with men, and hast prevailed. **30** And Jacob called the name of the place *Peniel (Face of God)*: for I have seen God face to face, and my life is preserved. (KJV)

❖ *Jacob became Israel when he struggled with God as Man!* ❖

Israel resists Jesus!

Israel is called "Jacob":

Jer 30:6 I see every man with his hands on his loins, as a woman in travail… **7** Alas! For that day is great, so that none is like it; it is even the time of *Jacob's trouble*; but he shall be saved out of it. (KJV)

❖ *Israel becomes Jacob when they struggle with Man (Jesus) as God!* ❖

Jacob was called Israel: he struggled with God as Man!	Israel is called Jacob: they struggle with Man as God!

Bloody City!

Princes shed blood:

Eze 22:2 Now, thou son of man, wilt thou judge the bloody city? Yea, thou shalt show her all her abominations. **6** Behold, the princes of Israel, everyone were in thee to their power to shed blood.
Micah 3:10 They (*Jacob/Israel*) build-up Zion with blood and Jerusalem with iniquity.
Rev 16:6 For they have shed the blood of *saints and prophets*, and Thou hast given them blood to drink… (KJV)

Cup of trembling!

Judah & Jerusalem under siege:

Zech 12:2 Behold, I will make *Jerusalem* a cup of trembling to all the people round about, when they *lay siege* both against *Judah* and against *Jerusalem*. **10** And I will pour upon the house of David, and upon the inhabitants of Jerusalem, the spirit of grace and of supplications: and they shall look upon Me whom they have pierced, and they shall mourn for Him, as one mourns for his only son, and shall be in bitterness for Him, as one that is in bitterness for his firstborn. (KJV)

The Lord pours His fury!

Israel calls on the LORD!

Eze 22:19 Thus says the Lord GOD; "Because ye are all become *dross (residue)*, behold, therefore I will gather you into the midst of Jerusalem." **22** As silver is melted in the midst of the furnace, so shall ye be melted in the midst thereof; and ye shall know that I the LORD have poured out My fury upon you.
Zech 13:9 And I will bring the 3rd *part* through the fire, and will refine them as silver is refined, and will try them as gold is tried: they shall call on *My Name (Jesus)*, and I will hear them: I will say, "It is My people": and they shall say, "*The LORD (Jesus) is my God*." (KJV)

❖ *After being tested they shall know that the LORD JESUS is GOD!* ❖

16. When will the Holy people have power? … (Pre) (Mid-week) (Post) … Page 31

FIVE OF 7 CHURCHES

~EPHESUS~ *Rev 2:1-7*

Revelation 2:3 You (*wise*) have persevered and have patience and have labored for My name's sake. **4** I have this against you, that you (*foolish*) have left your First Love. (**NKJ**)

Foolish: Thus, says the LORD unto (fallen) Israel, "Seek ye me, and ye shall live…" **Amos 5:4** (KJV)

~SMYRNA~ *Rev 2:8-11*

Rev 2:9 Those (*foolish*) who say they are Jews and are not; but are a synagogue of Satan. **10** The devil is about to throw some of you (*wise*) into prison, that you may be tested, and you will have tribulation 10 days. (**NKJ**)

~PERGAMOS~ *Rev 2:12-17*

Rev 2:13 You (*wise*) hold fast to My name (*Jesus*), and did not deny My faith. **14** (*foolish*) who hold the doctrine of Balaam, who taught Balak to put a stumbling block before the children of Israel, to eat things sacrificed... (**NKJ**)

Foolish: Israel, through the counsel of Balaam, (trespassed) against the Lord… **Num 31:16** (KJV)

~THYATIRA~ *Rev 2:18-29*

Rev 2:19 The (*wise*): I know your works, love, service, faith, and your patience…**20** That woman Jezebel, who calls herself a prophetess, (*teaches*) and (*seduces*) My (*foolish*) servants to commit sexual immorality and eat things sacrificed… (**NKJ**)

Foolish: Have forsaken the right way & gone astray, by following the doctrine of Balaam… **II Pet 2:15** (KJV)

~SARDIS~ *Rev 3:1-6*

Rev 3:1 I know your works, that you (*foolish*) have a name that you are alive, but you are dead. **4** You have a few names even in Sardis who have not defiled their garments; and they (*wise*) shall walk with Me in white, for they are worthy. (**NKJ**)

~PHILADELPHIA~ *Rev 3:7-13*

Kept from the Trial:

Rev 3:10 Because thou (***wise***) hast kept the word of my patience, I also will keep thee from the hour of temptation, which shall come upon all the world… (KJV)

*We shall all be changed, in a moment, in the twinkling of an eye… **I Cor 15:52** (KJV)*

❖ *"**Wise**" of first 5 churches will be taken with Philadelphia!* ❖

17. When will the church/believers be taken? … (Pre) (Mid-week) (Post) … Page 29

❖ <u>Christians/Believers</u> *will be gathered when the Lord sends His angels!* ❖

~LAODICEA~ *Rev 3:14-22*

Refined in Fire:

Rev 3:16 So then because thou (***foolish***) art lukewarm, and neither cold nor hot, I will spew thee out of my mouth. **18** I counsel thee to buy of me gold tried in the fire, that thou mayest be rich… (KJV)

*He that hath an ear, let him hear what the Spirit saith unto the (7) churches… **Rev 3:22** (KJV)*

❖ *"**Foolish**" of first 5 churches will be refined with Laodicea!* ❖

17. When will the church/remnant be taken? … (Pre) (Mid-week) (Post) … Page 30

❖ <u>Remnant</u> *who wait to accept Jesus will be tested for 3½ yrs.* ❖

PARABLE OF THE 10 VIRGINS!

Mat 25:10 the bridegroom came; and they (*5 wise virgins*) that were ready went in with Him to the marriage: and the door was shut. **11** Afterward came also the other (*5 foolish* virgins) saying, "Lord, Lord, open to us!" **12** But he answered and said, Verily I say unto you, I know you not. (KJV)

❖ *First 5 churches: "Wise" believers are anointed, but "foolish" non-believers will be tested!* ❖

❖ *10 Virgins: 5 "wise" virgins are taken, but 5 "foolish" virgins will be tested!* ❖

Another Beast!

Like a lamb: speaks as a dragon!
Revelation 13:11 And I beheld another beast coming up out of the earth; and he had *two horns like a lamb*, and he spoke as a dragon (*Satan*). (KJV)

*Satan himself is transformed into an angel of light.… **II Cor 11:14** (KJV)*

Power before the First beast!

Causes worship of the Beast:
Rev 13:12 And he (*False Prophet*) exercises all the power of the *"first beast" before him* and causes the earth and them which dwell therein to worship the first beast (*anti-Christ*), whose deadly wound was healed. **13** And he doeth great wonders, so that he makes fire come down from heaven on the earth in the sight of men. (KJV)

❖ *False Prophet: Another beast, lamb with 2 horns, also Shebna, Jezebel and Balaam* ❖

Deceives with signs:
Rev 13:14 And he (*F. Prophet*) deceived them that dwell on the earth by the means of those miracles which he had power to do in the sight of the (*first*) beast; saying to them that dwell on the earth, that they should make an image to the beast, which had the wound by a sword, and did live. **15** And he had power to give life unto the image of the beast, that the image of the beast should both speak, and cause that as many as would not worship the image of the beast should be killed. (KJV)

*Their torment ascends forever and ever; who worship the beast and his image ~ **Rev 14:11** (KJV)*

Mark needed to buy & sell!

Causes all to receive the mark:
Rev 13:16 And he (*False* Prophet) causes all, both small and great, rich and poor, free and bond, to receive a mark in their right hand, or in their foreheads, **17** that no man might *buy or sell*, save he that had the mark, or the name of the beast, or number of his name. **18** Here is wisdom. Let him that hath understanding count the number of the beast: for it is the number of a man; and his number is 6-6-6. (KJV)

❖ *Mid-week: Power of the dragon transfers from False Prophet to the anti-Christ!* ❖

Transfer of Power

Anti-Christ receives power of dragon:
Isa 22:15 Thus saith the Lord GOD of hosts, Go, get thee unto this treasurer, even unto *Shebna (False Prophet)*, which is over the house, and say, **19** I will drive thee from thy station, and from thy state shall he pull thee down. **20** And it shall come to pass in that day, that I will call my servant *Eliakim (Anti-Christ)* son of Hilkiah. **21** And I will clothe him with thy robe and strengthen him. (KJV)

❖ *Power-transfer from Shebna to Eliakim represents power-transfer from F. prophet to anti-Christ!* ❖

First Beast!

Beast with 7 heads & 10 horns:

Revelation 13:1 I stood upon the sand of the sea and saw a beast rise-up out of the sea, having 7 heads and *10 horns* (*tribes*), and upon his *horns 10 crowns* (*kingship*), and upon his heads the name of blasphemy. **2** And the beast which I saw was like unto a leopard, and his feet were as the feet of a bear, and his mouth as the mouth of a lion; and the dragon (*Satan*) gave him his power, and his seat, and great authority. (KJV)

And his power shall be mighty, but not by his own power! **Dan 8:24** (KJV)
❖ *Horns represent power, honor and glory; also, victory!* ❖

His mortal wound heals:

Rev 13:3 And I saw one of his heads as it were wounded to death; and his deadly wound was healed: and all the world wondered after the beast. **4** They worshipped the dragon which gave power unto the beast: and they worshipped the beast, saying, "Who is like unto the beast? Who is able to make war with him?" **6** Then he opened his mouth in blasphemy against God, to blaspheme His name, His tabernacle, and those who dwell in Heaven. (KJV)

❖ *10 Crowns represent kingship of the 10 dispersed/exiled tribes of Israel!* ❖

Power for 42 months!

Anti-Christ overcomes Saints:

Rev 13:5 And there was given unto him a mouth speaking great things and blasphemies; and *power* was given unto him to continue *42 mos*. **7** And it was given unto him to make war with the *saints*, and to *overcome* them: and power was given him over all kindreds, and tongues, and nations. **8** And all that dwell upon the earth shall worship him, whose names are not written in the Book of Life of the Lamb slain from the foundation of the world. **Dan 7:25** And he (*Little horn*) shall speak great words against the Most-High and shall wear out the *saints* of the Most-High and think to change times and laws: and they shall be given into his hand until (*3½ years*). (KJV)

❖ *Anti-Christ: First Beast, Little horn, Lawless one; also, Dan, Eliakim and king of Tyre!* ❖

18. When will Little horn make war with the saints? … (Pre) (Mid-week) (Post) … Page 31

❖ *The Beast is worshipped, but once his true intent is known, Israel resists him!* ❖

Key to House of David!

"Descendent" of Jacob:

Gen 49:16 "*Dan*" shall judge his people as one of the tribes of Israel. **17** "*Dan*" shall be a serpent by the way, an adder in the path that bites the horse heels so that his rider shall fall backward.
Isa 22:22 And the key of the house of David will I lay upon his shoulder; so, he (*Eliakim/Anti-Christ*) shall open, and none shall shut; and he shall shut, and none shall open. **23** And I will fasten him as a nail in a sure place; and he shall be for a glorious throne to his father's house. (KJV)

❖ *And he shall be a <u>father</u> to the inhabitants of Jerusalem, & to the house of Judah… Isa 22:21 (KJV)* ❖

Immanuel /God-with-us

Isa 7:14 Behold, a virgin shall conceive and bear a Son, and shall call His name *Immanuel*. **9:2** The people that walked in darkness have seen a Great Light; they that dwell in the land of the shadow of death, upon them hath the light shined. (KJV)

Almighty God (Son & Father)

Isa 9:6 For unto us a child is born, unto us a *"Son"* is given; the government shall be upon His shoulder: and His name shall be called Wonderful, Counsellor, The Mighty God, The Everlasting *"Father"*, The Prince of Peace.
Rev 1:8 I am the Alpha and the Omega, the Beginning and the End, says the Lord (*Jesus*), Which is, and Which was, and Which is to come, the Almighty. (KJV)

Holy One of Israel (Jesus)

Isa 10:17 And the light of Israel shall be for a fire, and his *Holy One* for a flame; **29:23** But when (*Jacob*) sees his children, the work of Mine hands, in the midst of (*Israel*), they shall sanctify *My Name*, and sanctify (*Jesus*) the *Holy One* of Jacob and shall fear the *God of Israel*. **47:4** As for our Redeemer, the LORD of hosts is His Name, the *Holy One* of Israel. (KJV)

❖ *Israel will sanctify Jesus as the Holy One of Jacob!* ❖

Holy Trinity of God!

Father, Son & Holy Spirit:
Isa 6:3 And one (*angel/seraphim*) cried unto another, and said, Holy (*Father*), Holy (*Son*), Holy (*Spirit*) is the LORD of hosts: the whole earth is full of his glory.
48:16 And now the Lord God (*Father*) and His (*Holy*) Spirit have sent Me (*Son*)… **17** Thus says the Lord, thy Redeemer, the Holy One of Israel: I am the Lord your God, which teaches thee to profit…
61:1 The (*Holy*) Spirit of the Lord (*Father*) God is upon Me (*Son*); because the Lord hath anointed Me to preach good tidings to the meek, to bind up the brokenhearted, to proclaim liberty to the captives (*of sin*) … (KJV)

*My God (Father), My God (Holy Spirit), why hast Thou forsaken Me (Son) ~**Ps 22:1** (KJV)*

The Salvation of God!

Light to the Gentiles!
Isa 49:6 Thou (*Jesus*) should be My Servant to raise up the tribes of Jacob, and to restore the preserved of Israel, I will also give Thee for a *Light* to the *"Gentiles"*, that Thou may be *"My salvation"* unto the end of the earth…

Israel waits for Salvation!
Gen 49:18 I (*Israel*) have waited for your salvation, O Lord!
Exo 15:2 The LORD is my strength and song, and He is become my salvation; He is my God.
Isa 49:5 And now says the LORD that formed me from the womb to be his Servant, to bring Jacob again to him, "Though Israel be not gathered, yet shall I be glorious in the eyes of the LORD…"
Ps 18:46 The LORD lives; and blessed be my Rock; let the God of my salvation be exalted. (KJV)

❖ *Jesus is a light to the gentiles and God's salvation to the world!* ❖

Immanuel!	Holy One of Israel!	Salvation to the Gentiles!
Image of God!	Holy Trinity of God!	Israel waits for Salvation!

Holy One: Jesus is limited!

Ps 78:21 So a fire was kindled against Jacob, and anger also came up against Israel; **22** because they believed not in God and trusted not in His Salvation. **41** Yea, they turned back and tempted God, and limited the *Holy One* of *Israel*. **89:18** For the LORD is our defense; and the Holy One of Israel is our King. (KJV)

❖ *The Holy One of Israel that they limit is Jesus, the Anointed!* ❖

The LAMB is slain!

Offering for Sin:

Isa 53:3 He is despised and rejected of men, a Man of sorrows and acquainted with grief. **5** But He was wounded for our transgressions, He was bruised for our iniquities; **7** And as a sheep before her shearers is dumb, so He opened not His mouth. **10** Yet it pleased the Lord to bruise Him; He hath put Him to grief: when thou shalt make His soul an offering for sin… **11** My righteous Servant (*shall*) justify many, for He shall bear their iniquities…
Rev 5:6 And I beheld, and, lo, in the midst of the throne and of the 4 beasts, and in the midst of the elders, stood a *"Lamb"* as it had been slain, having 7 horns and 7 eyes, which are the *7 Spirits of God* sent forth into all the earth. **12** Worthy is the *Lamb* that was slain to receive power, riches, wisdom, strength, honor, glory, and blessing. (KJV)

Behold the Lamb of God, which taketh away the sin of the world… **John 1:29** (KJV)

Wounded by His friends!
Psalm 22:16 The assembly of the wicked have enclosed Me; they *pierced My hands and My feet*. **32:1** Blessed is he *whose transgression is forgiven, whose sin is covered.*
Zech 13:6 And one shall say unto him, "What are these wounds in thine hands?" Then he shall answer, "Those with which I was *wounded* in the house of *My friends*". (KJV)

The Son of Man must suffer many things and be rejected… **Luke 9:22** (KJV)

God's salvation is forsaken!
Deut 32:15 Then (*Jeshurun/Israel*) forsook God which made him, and lightly esteemed the *Rock* of his Salvation… **17** They sacrificed unto devils, not to God; to gods whom they knew not … **18** Of the *Rock* that begat thee thou art unmindful, and hast *forgotten God* that formed thee. **28** For they are a nation void of counsel, neither is there any understanding in them. **36** For the LORD shall judge His people, and repent Himself for His servants… (KJV)

The Stone which the builders rejected has become the Chief Cornerstone… **Ps 118:22** (**NKJ**)

Redeemer: Jesus is despised!
Israel remains chosen:
Isa 49:7 Thus says the LORD, the *Redeemer of Israel, His Holy One* (*Jesus*), to whom man *despises*, to Him whom the nation (*Israel*) abhors, to a servant of rulers, kings shall see and arise, princes also shall worship, because of the LORD that is faithful, the *Holy One of Israel*; He shall *choose* thee.
Ps 51:12 Restore unto me the joy of Thy salvation; and uphold me with Thy Free Spirit. **14** Deliver me from blood-guiltiness, O God, thou God of my salvation: and my tongue shall sing aloud of thy righteousness. (KJV)

Blindness in part is happened to Israel, until the fullness of the Gentiles… **Rom 11:25** (KJV)

Salvation is rejected!	The Lamb is slain!	Redeemer/Jesus is despised!
Holy One/Jesus is limited!	Wounded by friends!	God's salvation is forsaken!

7 SEALS ARE OPENED

The Lamb opens the Seals!

Fourth of earth is killed:

Rev 6:1-8 *4 seals:* <u>White</u> horse to conquer, <u>red</u> horse takes peace from the earth, <u>black</u> horse brings hunger, <u>pale</u> horse: and his name that sat on him was *Death*, and *Hell* followed with him… And power was given unto them over the 4th part of the earth, to kill with *sword*, and with *hunger*, and with *death*, and with beasts of the earth. (KJV)

Souls slain for the Word:

Rev 6:9 *5th seal:* I saw under the altar the souls of them that were slain for the word of God, and for the testimony which they held. (KJV)

For Your sake we are killed all day long; …as sheep for the slaughter ~**Ps 44:22** (**NKJ**)

Stars of heaven fall:

Rev 6:12 *6th seal:* There was a great earthquake; and the sun became black as sackcloth of hair, and the moon became as blood. **13** And the stars of heaven fell to the earth… **15** Every bondman, and every free man, hid themselves in the dens and in the rocks of the mountains… (KJV)

Silence in Heaven!

144,000 are fed the Gospel:

Rev 8:1 *7th seal:* There was *silence in Heaven* about the space of half an hour. **12:6** And the *woman/144,000* fled into the wilderness, where she hath a place prepared of God, that they should "*feed*" her there *1,260 days*. **14** Into the wilderness, into her place, where she is "*nourished*" for *3½ years* from the face of the serpent… **14:3** and no man could learn that "*song/Gospel*" but the 144,000, which were redeemed from the earth. (KJV)

*And there were sealed 144,000 of all the tribes of Israel… **Rev 7:4** (KJV)*

19. What is the half-hour of silence in heaven? … Page 30

3 Trumpets: Star named "Wormwood"!

Rev 8:7 *1ˢᵗ trumpet*: Hail and fire mingled with blood, were cast upon the earth; a 3ʳᵈ part of trees burn-up.
***2ⁿᵈ trumpet*:** Great mountain burning with fire was cast into the sea… 3ʳᵈ part of the sea became blood…
***3ʳᵈ trumpet*:** And there fell a great star from heaven… upon the 3ʳᵈ part of the rivers. **11** And the name of the star is called "Wormwood": and the 3ʳᵈ part of the waters became wormwood, and many men died of the waters… (KJV)

3ʳᵈ of the days darken!

8:12 *4ᵗʰ trumpet*: The 3ʳᵈ *part* of the sun was smitten and the 3ʳᵈ *part* of the moon, and the 3ʳᵈ *part* of the stars, so as the 3ʳᵈ *part* of them was darkened, and the *day* shone not for a 3ʳᵈ part of it, and the night likewise. (KJV)

❖ ***Consider: 1,260 days, 42 months and 3½ years are the most-prophesied timelines!*** ❖

20. Which days will be darkened? … Page 32

Fallen angel opens pit of locusts:

Rev 9:2 *5ᵗʰ trumpet*: And he/fallen angel opened the *bottomless pit*; and there arose a smoke out of the pit… **3** And there came out of the smoke "*locusts*" upon the earth: **5** And to them it was given that they should not kill them (*men which have not the seal of God*), but that they should be tormented *five months*… (KJV)

Army of 200 million slays 3ʳᵈ of men:

Rev 9:15 *6ᵗʰ trumpet*: *4 angels* were prepared for an hour, and a day, and a month, and year, for to slay the 3ʳᵈ part of men. **16** And the number of the *army* of the horsemen was *200 million*; and I heard the number of them. **18** By these *three* was the 3ʳᵈ part of men killed: by the *fire*, and by the *smoke*, and by the *brimstone*… (KJV)

The Lord gives voice to "His army", for His camp is very great ~ **Joel 2:11** (KJV)

Bitter-sweet Book is "eaten:"

Rev 10:10 It (*little book*) was in my mouth *sweet* as honey: and as soon as I had "*eaten*" it, my belly was *bitter*. **11** And he said. "Thou must prophesy again before many peoples…" **12:6** And the woman/144,000 fled into the wilderness where she hath a place prepared of God, that they should "*feed*" her there 1,260 days. (KJV)

21. What is the bittersweet little book? … Page 33

Holy city is trampled 42 months!

Two witnesses prophesy 1,260 days:

Rev 11:2 The Holy city shall they/gentiles tread under foot *42 months*. **3** And I will give power unto My 2 witnesses (Elijah & Elisha), and they shall prophesy 1,260 days, clothed in sackcloth. (KJV)

Temple of God opens in Heaven!

The earth swallows the "flood":

Rev 11:19 *7ᵗʰ Trumpet*: The temple of God was opened in heaven, and there was seen in his temple the ark of his testament: and there were lightnings, and voices, and thunder, and an earthquake, and "*great hail*". **12:15** And the *serpent* cast out of his mouth water as a "*flood*" after the woman/Israel… **16** And the earth helped the *woman*, and the earth opened her mouth and swallowed the "*flood*" (locusts) which the dragon cast out of his mouth… (KJV)

Treasury of "hail" which I have reserved against the time of trouble… **Job 38:23** (KJV)
❖ ***Flood of "locusts" that were cast upon the earth return to the bottomless pit!*** ❖

144,000 are redeemed!

The "Gospel" is preached:

Rev 10:2 And he/Mighty Angel had in his hand a *"little book"* open… **8** "Go and take the *little book* which is open in the hand of the angel… **9** and it shall make thy belly *bitter*, but it shall be in thy mouth *sweet* as honey".

Rev 14:3 They (*144,000*) sang as it were a *"new song"* before the Throne, and before the 4 beasts, and the elders: and no man could learn that *"song"* but the *144,000* which were redeemed from the earth. **14:6** I saw another…

1ˢᵗ Angel in the midst of Heaven, having the *Everlasting Gospel to preach* unto them that dwell on the earth… (KJV)

22. When will the "Gospel" be preached? … (Pre) (Mid-week) (Post) … Page 33

Babylon is fallen!

Nations drink of her wrath:

Rev 14:8 **2ⁿᵈ angel:** And there followed another *angel*, saying, Babylon is fallen, is fallen, that great city, because she made all nations drink of the wine of the wrath of her fornication. (KJV)

Come out of (Babylon), My people, that ye be not partakers of her sins… **Rev 18:4** (KJV)

The mark brings torment:

Rev 14:9 The **3ʳᵈ angel** followed them saying, with a loud voice, if any man worships the beast and his image, and receive his mark in his forehead, or in his hand… **10** The same shall drink of the wine of the wrath of God… **11** And the smoke of their torment ascends-up forever and ever… (KJV)

And they worshipped the dragon… and they worshiped the beast… **Rev 13:4** (KJV)

Harvest of the earth:

Rev 14:14 **4ᵗʰ angel:** And I looked, and behold a white cloud, and upon the cloud one sat *like unto* the *Son of man (Angel of the Lord)*, having on his head a golden crown, and in his hand a *sharp sickle*.

14:15 **5ᵗʰ angel:** And another angel came out of the temple, crying with a loud voice to him that sat on the cloud, "Thrust in thy sickle, and reap; for the time is come for thee to reap; for the *harvest of the earth* is ripe." (KJV)

The Winepress is trodden!

Blood reaches horses' bridles:

Rev 14:17 **6ᵗʰ angel:** And *another angel* came out of the temple which is in Heaven, he also having a *sharp sickle*. **14:18** **7ᵗʰ angel:** And *another angel* cried with a loud cry to him that had the *sharp sickle*, saying, "Thrust in thy *sharp sickle*, and gather the clusters of the vine of the earth; for her grapes are fully ripe." **20** And the *winepress* was trodden outside the city, and blood came out of the *winepress*, even unto the horses' bridles, by the space of 1,600 furlongs. (KJV)

The indignation of the LORD is upon all nations, and his fury upon all their armies… **Isa 34:2** (KJV)

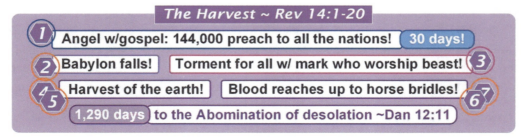

Victory over the beast!

Song of Moses & Song of the Lamb:

Revelation 15:2 Them that had gotten the *victory over the beast*, over his image, over his mark, and over the number of his name, **3** sing the *song (law)* of Moses, the servant of God, and *song (Gospel)* of the Lamb. (KJV)

*The LORD is my strength & "song", and He is become my Salvation: He is my God… **Exo 15:2** (KJV)*

God's glory fills temple

No one enters temple:

Rev 15:8 And the temple was filled with smoke from the glory of God, and from His power; and no man was able to enter-into the temple, till the 7 plagues of the 7 angels were fulfilled. (KJV)

*"I will fill this house/temple with glory, saith the LORD of hosts…" **Hag 2:7** (KJV)*

4 Vials (Bowls or Plagues)

Power of God's Name:

Rev 16:2 <u>*1st vial*</u> *upon the earth*: and there fell a noisome and grievous sore upon the men which had the mark of the beast, and upon them which worshipped his image.

16:3 <u>*2nd vial*</u> *upon the sea*: and it became as the blood of a dead man; and every living soul died in the sea.

16:4 <u>*3rd vial*</u> *upon the rivers and springs of water*: and they became blood. **6** For they (*which had the mark of the beast*) have shed the blood of saints and prophets, and thou hast given them blood to drink; for they are worthy.

16:8 <u>*4th vial*</u> *upon the sun*: and power was given unto him to scorch men with fire. **9** And men were scorched with great heat and blasphemed the *Name of God*, which hath power over these *plagues*: and they repented not to give Him (*Jesus*) glory. (KJV)

Final 3 Vials!

God remembers Babylon:

16:10 <u>*5th vial*</u> *upon the seat of the beast*: his kingdom was full of darkness; and they gnawed their tongues for pain.

16:12 <u>*6th vial*</u> *upon the great river Euphrates*: and the water thereof was dried up, that the way of the kings of the east might be prepared. **14** For they are the (*3 unclean*) spirits of devils, working miracles, which go forth unto the kings of the earth and of the whole world, to gather them to the battle of that great Day of God Almighty.

16:17 <u>*7th vial*</u> *into the air*: **18** And there was a great earthquake, such as was not since men were upon the earth… **19** The great city ("*Mystery, Babylon*") was divided into 3 *parts* and the cities of the nations fell, and *great Babylon came in remembrance before God*, to give unto her the cup of the wine of the fierceness of His wrath. (KJV)

24. Where will "Mystery, Babylon" be found? … Page 35

---

7 Plagues ~ Rev 15 & 16

No one enters temple till 7 plagues fulfill God's wrath ~*Rev 15:8*

Foul sores upon men with mark who worship Beast & image! ①

②③ Waters bloodied for saints & prophets! | Sun scorches men! ④

Kingdom & seat of beast fill with darkness & with pain! ⑤

⑥ Armageddon: Euphrates dries up! Babylon: great quake & hail! ⑦

JUDGMENTS

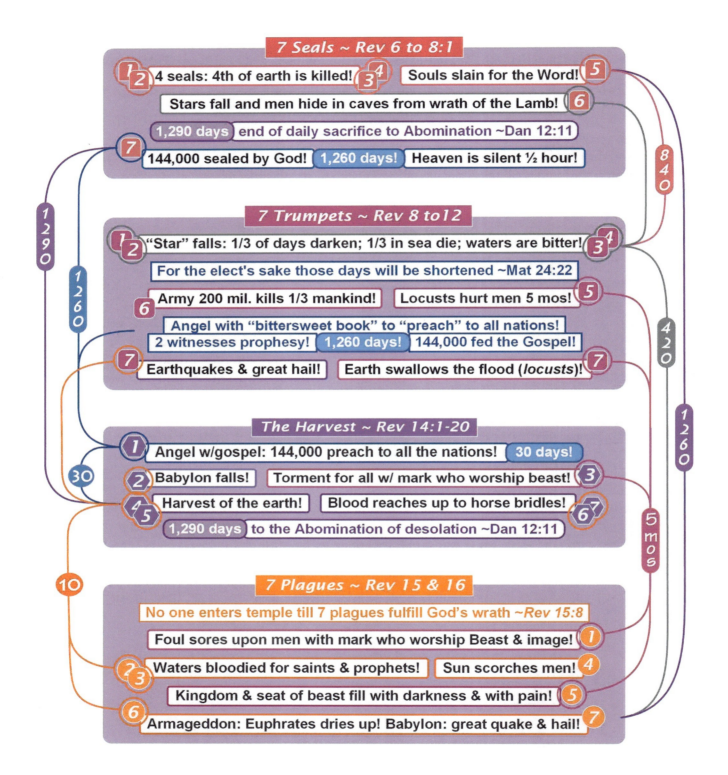

ANSWER & OVERVIEW SECTION

This Section presents the End-time events in Chronological order!

SIGNS OF HIS COMING

The first half of the tribulation is marked by deception and a falling away. Israel returns to captivity when they reinstate the sacrificial system. This uncovers their sins before God, because of their denial of Jesus as their Savior. Devious "peace" and rejoicing will blind the world to the great tribulation that is soon to come!

ANOTHER BEAST   Page 25

* Who devises the covenant that anti-Christ confirms?

TEMPLE AND THE "WALL"   Page 26

* When will the temple and "wall" be built?

THE FALLING AWAY   Page 27

* What is the falling away that comes first?

ISRAEL IS DECEIVED   Page 28

* How will prophets deceive Israel?
* Why does Israel return to "captivity"?

MID-WEEK

Half-way through the tribulation period, the restrainer of Satan is taken away. The anti-Christ is revealed when he receives the power of Satan and abolishes the sacrificial system. On the Day of His Coming, the Lord appears on the clouds of heaven for all to see. His glory will obscure the heavens and the earth will mourn when all "believers" are taken!

DAY OF HIS COMING   Page 29

* When will be the Day of His Coming?
* When will Angels gather the elect?
* When will the church/Believers be taken?

"Signs of the End" that follow, are also known as the "Day of the Lord" or "Jacob's Trouble"!

ANSWER & OVERVIEW SECTION

SIGNS OF THE END

The Lord will leave the Anti-Christ with "absolute power" during the final 3 ½ years! During the Great Tribulation, God will use the siege of Jerusalem to judge the nations with the army of the Lord!

DAY OF THE LORD   Page 30

- How long will be the day of the Lord?
- When will the church/remnant be taken?
- What is the half-hour of silence in Heaven?

LITTLE HORN/ANTI CHRIST   Page 31

- Who restrains the "lawlessness" of Satan?
- When will the Little horn enter Jerusalem?
- When will the Holy people have power?
- When will the Little horn make war with the saints?

DAYS OF PERSECUTION   Page 32

- How will the 1,260 days of persecution be shortened?
- Which days will be darkened?
- Why did God allow Satan to torment Job?

THE 144,000 ARE "FED"   Page 33

- What is the "Bittersweet Little Book"?
- When will the Gospel be preached?
- Who will have tribulation 10 days?

TIME OF TROUBLE   Page 34

- How will the end be with a flood?
- When will armies surround Jerusalem?
- When will the Abomination be set-up?

MYSTERY, BABYLON   Page 35

- Where will Mystery, Babylon be found?

The Day of Wrath

The Lord will reveal Himself and the enemies of Israel will be consumed in God's wrath! Jesus will stand upon the Mount of Olives a second time, to recover the remnant of His people and make a new covenant with Israel.

ANOTHER BEAST

False Prophet deceives!

F. Prophet has power first!

Rev 13:12 And he (*F. Prophet*) exercises all the *power* of the *1ˢᵗ beast* <u>before</u> him…

Zech 11:16 For, lo, I will raise up a *shepherd* (*False Prophet*) in the land, which shall not visit those that be cut off… **17** Woe to the idol (*worthless*) shepherd that leaves the flock! The sword shall be upon his arm, and his right eye: his arm shall be clean dried-up, and his right eye shall be utterly darkened.

I Kings 22:17 (*Micaiah*) said, I saw all Israel scattered upon the hills, as sheep that have *not a shepherd*; and the LORD said, "These have *no Master*: let them return every man to his house in peace." (KJV)

Covenant with Death!

Agreement with Hell:

Jer 23:14 I have seen also in the *prophets of Jerusalem* a horrible thing: they commit adultery, and *walk in lies*: they strengthen also the hands of evildoers, that *none doth return* from his wickedness…

Isa 28:15 Ye have said, "We have made a *covenant* with *Death*, and with *Hell* are we at agreement…" **18** And your *covenant* with *Death* shall be disannulled, and your agreement with *Hell* shall not stand… (KJV)

---

3. Who "*devises*" the covenant that anti-Christ confirms? (Page 1)

Doctrine of Balaam: "*Things sacrificed*"!

Rev 2:14 (*You*) hold the doctrine of *Balaam* (*False Prophet*), who taught Balac to cast a *stumbling-block* before the children of Israel, to eat "*things sacrificed*" unto idols… **20** You suffer that woman *Jezebel* (*False Prophet*), who calls herself a *prophetess*, to teach and to seduce My servants to commit fornication, and to eat *things sacrificed*… (KJV)

❖ **Things sacrificed: Blood of animals being used in sacrifice to cover sin!** ❖
Righteousness and justice are more acceptable to the Lord than <u>sacrifice</u>… **Pro 21:3**

3. The covenant will be "devised" by … … the False Prophet!

❖ **Doctrine of Balaam: Israel sins by rejecting the blood of Jesus to cover sin!** ❖

Jesus is a Sanctuary!

God prefers mercy, not sacrifice!

Isa 8:14 And He shall be for a *sanctuary*; but for a *stone of stumbling* and for a *rock of offence* to both the houses of Israel. **28:16** Therefore thus saith the Lord GOD, Behold, I lay in Zion for a foundation a Stone, a tried Stone, a precious Cornerstone, a sure foundation: he that believeth shall not make haste.

Hos 6:6 For I desired "*mercy*", and "*not sacrifice*"; and the knowledge of God more than burnt offerings. (KJV)

Anti-Christ: power 42 months!

Rev 13:5 There was given unto him (*anti-Christ*) a mouth speaking great things and blasphemies; *power* was given unto him to continue *42 months*.

Isa 22:20 I will call my servant Eliakim (*anti-Christ*) the son of Hilkiah: **21** And I will clothe him with thy robe, and strengthen him with thy girdle and I will commit thy (*F. Prophet's*) government into his hand… (KJV)

❖ *Power of dragon transfers from F. Prophet to anti-Christ for the final 42 months!* ❖

F. Prophet: power before First Beast!	Another Beast ~ Doctrine of Balaam!	Anti-Christ power last 42 months!
	"Stumbling" for Israel: "Things sacrificed"	
	Jesus is a Sanctuary: God prefers mercy!	

"Wall": altar to sin!

Isa 9:9 *Ephraim* and the inhabitant of *Samaria* (*10 tribes*), say in the *pride* and stoutness of heart... **10** The bricks are fallen-down, but we will *build* with *hewn stones*: the sycamores are cut down, but we will *change them*...

Hosea 8:11 Because *Ephraim* hath made many *altars to sin*, altars shall be unto him (*altar*) to sin.

We have made lies our refuge, and under falsehood have we hid ourselves... Isa 28:15 (KJV)

❖ *Wall of lies: sin-altar of unneeded animal-sacrifice!* ❖

I. **When will the temple & "wall" be built? (Pre) (Mid-week) (Post) (Page 1)**

"Wall": inside the temple!

Dan 9:25 To restore and to build *Jerusalem* unto Messiah the Prince shall be 7 and 62 weeks; the street shall be built again, and the *"wall"*, even in troublous times.

Zech 6:15 They (*10 exiled tribes*) that are far off, shall come and build <u>in</u> the temple of the LORD... (KJV)

❖ *The "altar of sacrifice" becomes a "wall" between Israel and God ~Eze 43:8* ❖

I. The temple and "wall" will be built ... ... (Pre)

Name of JESUS is profaned!

Animal blood profanes:

Mal 1:11 My Name shall be great among the heathen, saith the LORD of hosts. **12** But ye profaned it...

Lev 22:32 Neither shall ye profane My Holy Name; but I will be hallowed among Israel's children.

❖ *Substituting the blood of Jesus with blood of animals profanes His Holy Name!* ❖

"Un-tempered Wall" is fallen:

Eze 13:12 Lo, when the "wall" is fallen, "Where is the *daubing...?*" **13** There shall be an overflowing shower in Mine anger, and *"great hailstones"* in my fury to consume it. **14** So will I break down the *"wall"* that ye have *daubed* with <u>un-tempered mortar</u> and bring it down to the ground so that the foundation thereof shall be discovered, and it shall fall, and ye shall know that *I (JESUS) AM THE LORD...* **15** Thus will I accomplish My wrath upon the *"wall"*; and upon them that have *daubed* it. **43:8** The *"wall"* between Me and them/Israel: they have even *defiled* My Holy Name by their abominations that they have committed; wherefore I have consumed them in Mine anger. (KJV)

Treasures of the hail which I have reserved against the time of trouble... Job 38:23 (KJV)

The BRANCH builds His Temple

We are the Temple of God:

Zech 6:12 Behold, the *Man* (*Jesus*) whose name is: *The BRANCH*; and He shall grow up out of His place (*Heaven*), and He shall build the *"Temple of the Lord"*.

I Cor 3:16 Know ye not that ye are the *"Temple of God"*, and that the Spirit of God dwelleth in you? (KJV)

❖ *The Spiritual Temple that the BRANCH builds requires no sacrifice!* ❖

	Temple & the "Wall"		
<u>Altar to Sin:</u> "wall" between Israel & God!	<u>Blood of animals</u> profanes Jesus!	We are "temple the BRANCH builds!"	<u>Un-tempered</u> "wall" is fallen!

Israel is fallen!

Rev 2:2 I know thy works, thy labor, and patience... **4** Nevertheless I have somewhat against thee, because thou hast left thy *First Love*. **5** Remember therefore from whence thou art *fallen*, and repent and do the first works...
Deu 32:15 Then he (*Jeshurun/Israel*) *forsook God* which made him, and lightly esteemed the *Rock* of his *salvation*...
Amos 5:2 The virgin of *Israel* is *fallen*; she shall no more rise: she is *forsaken* upon her land...
Jer 8:5 Why then is this people of *Jerusalem sliding back* by a perpetual *backsliding*?

❖ *Falling away*: Israel backslides by forsaking God's salvation in Jesus! ❖

---

4. **What is the "falling away" that comes first? (Page 2)**

Israel backslides!

Isa 1:4 Ah sinful nation, a people laden with iniquity, a seed of evildoers, children that are corrupters, they have *forsaken the LORD*, they have provoked the Holy One of Israel unto anger, they are gone away *backward*.
Jer 3:12 Return, thou *backsliding* Israel, says the LORD; I will not cause mine anger to fall upon you. **14:7** O LORD (*JESUS*), though our iniquities testify against us, do Thou it for *Thy Name's sake*: for our *backslidings* are many; we have sinned against Thee.

4. The "falling away" is ... ... the "backsliding" of Israel!

Israel/Judah play the Harlot!

Israel: backsliding "heifer":

Jer 3:6 Has thou seen that which *backsliding Israel* hath done? She is gone up upon every high mountain and under every green tree, and there hath played the *Harlot*. **8** Yet her treacherous sister *Judah* feared not, but went and played the *Harlot* also...
Hos 4:15 Though thou, *Israel*, play the *Harlot*, yet let not *Judah* offend... **16** For Israel slides back as a *"backsliding heifer"*: now the LORD will feed them as a *"lamb"* in a large place. (KJV)

❖ *They will be fed as "lambs" for not accepting JESUS as the "LAMB"!* ❖

JESUS is a Sanctuary!

Stumbling Stone for Israel:

Isa 8:13 Sanctify the LORD of hosts Himself; let Him be your fear; and let Him be your dread. **14** And He (*Jesus*) shall be for a *"Sanctuary"*; but for a *"Stone of stumbling"* and for a *Rock of offense* to both the houses of *Israel*, for a gin and for a snare to the inhabitants of *Jerusalem*. **15** And many among them shall stumble, and fall, and be broken, and be snared, and be taken.

"Israel" is engraved in His palms:

Isa 49:6 I will also give Thee (*Jesus*) for a *light to the Gentiles*, that thou mayest be My Salvation unto the end of the earth. **15** Yea, they may forget, yet I will not forget thee. **16** Behold, I have engraved *thee/Zion* upon the palms of My hands. (KJV)

Falling Away!

| Israel has fallen: Backsliding heifer! | Israel/Judah play Harlots! | Jesus is a Sanctuary! Israel's Stumbling stone! | "Israel/Zion" is engraved! |

6. *How will prophets deceive Israel? (Page 4)*

Prophets promise "Peace"!

"Un-tempered" Mortar:
Jer 5:31 The prophets prophesy falsely, and the priests bear rule by their means; My people love to have it so. **8:11** For they have healed the hurt of the daughter of My people slightly, saying, *"Peace, peace!"* When there is *no peace*. **Eze 13:10** Because, even because they (*prophets*) have seduced my people, saying, Peace; and there was no peace; and one built up a *"wall"*, and, lo, others daubed it with *un-tempered* mortar: **11** O great hailstones, shall fall; and a stormy wind shall rend it… (see *Job 38:22-23*) (KJV)

> 6. Prophets deceive Israel … saying "Peace" but there is no peace!

God is blamed!

Prophets shall be consumed:
Jer 4:10 Then said I, Ah, Lord GOD! "Surely *Thou hast greatly deceived* this people and Jerusalem, saying, Ye shall have peace; whereas the sword reaches the soul". **14:15** Therefore, thus says the LORD concerning the prophets that prophesy in *My name*, and *I sent them not*, yet they say, sword and famine shall not be in this land; by *"sword and famine"* those *prophets* shall be consumed. (KJV).

> *Yet will I (Jesus) be to (Israel) as a "little sanctuary" in the countries where they shall come… Eze 11:16*

15. *Why does Israel return to "captivity"? (Page 10)*

No trust in Christ's blood!

Captivity of (un-covered) sin:
Lam 2:14 (*thy prophets*) have not revealed thy iniquity, to turn away thy (*sin*) captivity…
Eze 21:24 Ye have made your *iniquity/sin* to be *remembered* in that your transgressions are *discovered/uncovered*…
Ps 4:2 O ye sons of men, how long will ye turn My glory into shame? **5** Offer the sacrifices of righteousness and put your trust in the LORD (*JESUS*). (KJV)

> *If the "blood" of bulls and goats sanctifies, …how much more the "blood" of Christ? Heb 9:13-14 (KJV)*

> 15. Israel returns to "captivity" … … by returning to the bondage of "sin" sacrifice!
> ❖ *Prophets and priests will be held accountable for not exposing Israel's sin!* ❖

No Trust in God's Salvation!

"Forgotten sin" is remembered:
Isa 23:15 And it shall come to pass in that day, that *Tyre/Jerusalem* shall be forgotten *70 years*… **17** And it shall come to pass *after* the end of *70 years*, that the LORD will *visit/remember* Tyre…
Ps 22:29 All they that go down to the dust shall bow before Him (*Jesus*): and none can keep alive his own soul.
Ps 78:22 Because they (*Jacob/Israel*) believed not in God, and trusted not in *His salvation*.
Jer 14:10 (*The Lord/Jesus*) will now *remember* their iniquity, and *visit their sins*… (KJV)

> *Now is come <u>salvation</u>, and the kingdom of our <u>God</u>, and the power of <u>His Christ</u>… Rev 12:10 (KJV)*

	Israel is deceived!	
Blood of Jesus covers sin!		Animal blood uncovers sin!
Un-tempered wall is un-covered sin!		Their forgotten sin is remembered!

❖ *Blood of animals <u>uncovers</u> sin that was covered by the blood of Jesus!* ❖

---

7. **When will be the Day of His coming? ... (Pre) (Mid-week) (Post) ... (Page 4)**

The Glory of the Lord!

Rev 1:7 Behold, He cometh with *"clouds"*; and *every eye shall see Him* and they also which pierced Him: and all kindreds of the earth shall wail because of Him. Even so, Amen.

1 The 4:17 Then we which are alive and remain shall be *"caught-up together"* with them (*the dead in Christ*) in the clouds, to meet the Lord in the air: and so, shall we ever be with the Lord... (KJV)

> **7. The Day of His coming will be ... ...** (Mid-week)
> ❖ *The brightness of His glory will overwhelm the heavenly lights!* ❖

---

8. **When will Angels gather the elect? ... (Pre) (Mid-week) (Post) ... (Page 4)**

Angels gather His elect:

Mat 24:31 And He shall send His angels with a great sound of a trumpet, and they will gather together His elect from the four winds, from one end of heaven to the other. (KJV)

> **8. Angels will gather the elect ... ...** (Mid-week)

---

17. **When will the "church/believers" be taken? ... (Pre) (Mid-week) (Post) ... (Page 13)**

Philadelphia kept from the trial:

Rev 3:8 ~ 6th *church* ~ Thou (*Philadelphia*) has a *"little strength"*, has kept My word, and has not denied My name. **10** Because thou hast kept the word of my patience, I also will keep thee from the hour of temptation, which shall come upon all the world, to try them that dwell upon the earth.

Mat 25:10 The bridegroom came; and they that were ready went in with him to the marriage... (KJV)

> **17. Church/Philadelphia will be taken ... ...** (Mid-week) (also see Pg. 30)
> ❖ *The Church is not the "restrainer" because it will have "little strength"* ❖

The restrainer is taken!

The man of Sin is revealed:

2 The 2:7 Only he (*Michael*) who now "restrains" (*lawlessness*) will do so until he is taken out of the way...

8 And then shall the wicked be revealed... (**NKJ**)

Rev 12:12 The *devil* is come down unto you, having great wrath, because he knows he hath but a *"short time..."*

And he was given authority to continue for 42 months.... Rev 13:5

> **Mid-week: Day of His coming!**
> "Restrainer" is taken away! | Philadelphia is taken! | Man of sin is revealed!

❖ *The Holy Spirit is not the "restrainer" because God cannot be taken away!* ❖

DAY OF THE LORD

---

10. **How long will be the day of the Lord? (Page 6)**

Time of the gentiles!
Isa 13:6 Wail, for the *day of the LORD* is at hand! It will come as destruction from the *Almighty*.
Eze 30:3 Even the day of the Lord is near; it shall be the time of the heathen/gentiles …
Rev 11:2 And the Holy city shall they (*gentiles*) tread under foot *42 months*… (KJV)

10. The day of the Lord will last … … 42 months
❖ *Jerusalem will be trampled 42 months because they trampled the blood of Jesus!* ❖

---

17. **When will the church/remnant be taken? … (Pre) (Mid-week) (Post) … (Page 13)**

Laodicea will be refined 3½ years:
Dan 7:25 And they (*saints*) shall be given into his (*Little horn's*) hand until 3½ years…
Zech 13:9 And I will bring the 3rd part through the fire, and will refine them as silver is refined…
Rev 3:18 I counsel thee (*Laodicea*) to buy from Me gold tried in fire, that thou may be rich; and white raiment, that thou may be clothed; anoint thine eyes with eye salve, that you may see.
Rev 6:9 (*5th Seal*) I saw under the altar the souls of them that were slain for the word of God…(KJV)

17. Church/Laodicea will be "refined" … … (Post)
❖ *Church/Laodicea will be "tested" after Philadelphia has been taken* ❖

---

19. **What is half-hour of silence in Heaven? (Page 18)**

No answer from God!
Amos 8:11 I will send a famine in the land, not a famine of bread, nor a thirst for water, but of *"hearing the words of the Lord"*. **12** They shall run to-and-fro to seek the Word of the LORD…
Isa 29:10 For the LORD has poured out upon you the spirit of deep sleep and has closed your eyes; namely, the prophets; and He has covered your heads, namely, the seers.
Micah 3:7 Then shall the seers be ashamed, and the diviners confounded: yea, they shall all cover their lips; for there is *no answer of God*. (KJV)

19. Half-hour silence in Heaven is … … no word from God for the final 1,260 days!

	Day of the Lord!	
Laodicea: church refined 3½ years!	*42 months: Time of gentiles!*	*Half-hour silence: no answer from God!*

❖ *Day of the Lord: from His appearing in the air until He stands on Mount of Olives!* ❖

The "Book" is sealed!
Exo 15:2 The LORD is my strength and *"song"*, and He is become my salvation; He is my God.
Isa 29:11 And the vision of all is become unto you as the *"words* of a *book* that is *sealed"*, which men deliver to one that is learned, saying, "Read this"' and he said, "I cannot; for it is sealed".
Rev 14:3 And no man could learn that *"song"* but the *144,000* which were redeemed from the earth… (KJV)

❖ *The "Book" that is sealed: The "Word" of the Lord that only the 144,000 can learn!* ❖

5 *Who restrains the "lawlessness" of Satan? (Page 2)*

Restrainer is taken:

Rev 12:7 Michael and his angels fought against the dragon; and the *dragon* fought and his angels, **8** and prevailed not; neither was their place found any more in Heaven.

II The 2:7 Until he (*restrainer*) is taken out of the way... **8** And then (*anti-Christ*) will be revealed...

Rev 13:2 The *dragon* gave him (*beast*) his *power*, his *throne*, and great authority. (KJV)

> **5. The "lawlessness" of Satan is restrained by ... ... Archangel Michael**
> ❖ *Without Michael, anti-Christ receives power & throne of the dragon!* ❖

---

14. *When will the Little horn enter Jerusalem? ... (Pre) (Mid-week) (Post) ... (Page 9)*

Satan enters Little Horn:

Dan 8:9 And out of one of them (*4 horns*) came forth a *little horn*, which waxed exceeding great, toward the south, and toward the east, and toward the pleasant land (*Judah*).**10** And it grew up to the host of Heaven; and it cast down some of the host and some of the *stars* (*fallen angels*) to the ground and (*it*) trampled them.

Lam 4:12 The kings of the earth, and all inhabitants of the world, would not have believed that the adversary (*Satan*) and the enemy (*anti-Christ*) could "*enter*" the gates of *Jerusalem*. (KJV)

> **14. The Little horn will "enter" Jerusalem ... ... (Mid-week)**

---

16. *When will Holy people have power? ... (Pre) (Mid-week) (Post) ... (Page 11)*

3½ years: Holy people have power!

Dan 12:7 And (*the man clothed in linen*) swore by him that lives forever that it shall be for (*3½ years*); and when he (*anti-Christ*) shall have accomplished to scatter the power of the *Holy people*, all these things shall be *finished*...

Rev 10:7 (*7th trumpet*): The mystery of God should be *finished*, as he declared to his servants the prophets... (KJV)

> **16. The "Holy People" will have power ... ... (Post)!**

---

18. *When will Little horn make war with the saints? ... (Pre) (Mid-week) (Post) ... (Page 15)*

42 months: Little horn overcomes Israel!

Rev 13:1 And I stood upon the sand of the sea and saw a beast (*anti-Christ*) rise-up out of the sea, having *7 heads* and *10 horns* (*tribes*), and upon his horns *10 crowns* (*kingship*), and upon his heads the name of blasphemy. **5** And there was given unto him a mouth speaking great things and blasphemies, and power was given unto him to continue "*42 months*". **7** And it was given unto him to make war with the saints (*Israel*), and to *overcome* them...

Dan 7:25 He (*Little horn*) shall speak great words against the Most-High; and shall wear out the saints of the Most-High and think to change times and laws; and they (*10 tribes*) shall be given into his hand (*3½ years*). (KJV)

> **18. Little horn will war with the saints/Israel ... ... (Post)**
> ❖ <u>**10 horns:**</u> *10 tribes shall battle against anti-Christ during the final 3½ years!* ❖

| Michael is taken! | **Little horn / 3 ½ yrs - 42 mos!** | Power of Holy people! |
| Lit. horn has power! | Little horn enters Jerusalem! | Israel is overcome! |

DAYS OF PERSECUTION

1,260 days become 840!

Souls slain for the Word of God:
Rev 6: 9 (*5ᵗʰ Seal*) I saw under the altar the souls of them that were slain for the word of God... (KJV)

> **9.** How will the 1,260 days of persecution be shortened? (Page 5)

Stars fall & the sun darkens!
Rev 6:12 (*6ᵗʰ Seal*) Lo, there was a great earthquake; and the sun became black as sackcloth of hair, and the moon became like blood. **13** The stars of heaven fell unto the earth... **15** And every bondman, and every free man, hid themselves in the dens and in the rocks of the mountains; (KJV)

> **9. Persecution is shortened ... ... when a 3ʳᵈ of the 1,260 days are darkened!**
> *Except those days should be shortened, there should no flesh be saved...* **Mat 24:22** (KJV)

> **20.** Which days will be darkened? (Page 19)

420 days of darkness:
Rev 8:12 (*4ᵗʰ trumpet*) And a 3ʳᵈ of the sun was struck, a 3ʳᵈ of the moon, and a 3ʳᵈ of the stars, so that a 3ʳᵈ of them were darkened. A "3ʳᵈ of the day" (*420 days*) did not shine, and likewise "*the night*". (**NKJ**)

> **20. The days that will be darkened are ... ... one-third of 1,260 days, or 420 days!**

840 days: slain for the Word! (5th seal)	**Persecution: 3½ yrs. (1,260 days)**	**390-day siege!**
	420 days darken! (4th trumpet)	**40 days: for iniquity!**

390-day siege of Jerusalem:
Eze 4:5 For I have laid upon thee (*Ezekiel*) the years of their iniquity, according to the number of the days: "*390 days*"; so, shalt thou bear the iniquity of the house of Israel.

❖ **390-day siege: for 390 years of the iniquity of Israel!** ❖

40 years of iniquity:
Num 14:33 Your children shall wander in the wilderness *40 years* and bear your whoredoms. **34** After the number of days in which ye searched the land, even 40 days...
Mat 24:14 This Gospel of the kingddom shall be preached in all the world (*30 days*), then shall the end come...
Rev 2:10 The devil shall cast some of you into prison that ye may be tried; and you will have tribulation (*10 days*).
Eze 4:6 And thou shalt bear the iniquity of the house of Judah 40 days... (KJV)

❖ **40 days: The Gospel is preached 30 days & they suffer tribulation 10 days!** ❖

> **23.** Why did God allow Satan to torment Job? (Page 32)

Job 1:8 Then the LORD said unto Satan, "Hast thou considered my servant Job (*Israel*), that there is none like him in the earth, a perfect and an upright man (*Nation*), one that fears God..." (KJV)

> **23. As God allowed the torment of Job so will He allow the torment of Israel!**

21. What is the "Bittersweet Little Book"? (Page 19)

They are "fed" 1,260 days:

Rev 12:6 And the woman (*144,000*) fled into the wilderness, where she hath a place prepared of God, that they should "feed" her (*the Gospel*) there 1,260 days. **12:14** And to the woman were given two wings of a great eagle, that she might fly into the wilderness, into her place, where she is nourished for (*3½ years*), from the face of the serpent. **14:6** And I saw another angel fly in the midst of heaven, having the "*Everlasting Gospel*" to preach unto them that dwell on the earth, and to every nation, kindred, tongue, and people. (KJV)

The LORD is my strength and "song", and He is become my Salvation…~ **Exo 15:2** (KJV)

21. The "Bittersweet Little Book" is … … the "Everlasting Gospel"

❖ *The "Gospel" is sweet but learning too late makes it bitter!* ❖

---

22. When will the Gospel be preached? (Page 20)

Everlasting "Gospel/Song":

Rev 14:3 And they sung as it were a "*new song*" before the throne, and before the 4 beasts, and the elders and no man could learn that "*song*" but the 144,000, which were redeemed from the earth.

Isa 29:18 And in that day, shall the deaf hear the words of the book, and the eyes of the blind shall see out of obscurity, and out of darkness. **52:7** How beautiful upon the mountains are the feet of him that brings good tidings, that publishes peace; that brings good tidings of good, that publishes salvation; that says unto Zion, "Thy God reigns!" (KJV)

They sing the "song (law)" of Moses, and the "song (Gospel)" of the Lamb~ **Rev 15:3** (KJV)

Gospel is preached before the end:

Mat 24:14 And this *gospel* of the kingdom shall be preached in all the world (*30 days*) for a witness unto all nations, and then shall the *end come.* (KJV)

22. The Gospel will be preached … … 30 days before the end!

❖ *The 144,000 are fed the Gospel 1,260 days & they preach 30 days (1,290 days)* ❖

---

13. Who will have tribulation 10 days? (Page 8)

144,000 are sealed:

Rev 2:10 Behold, the devil shall cast some of you into prison, that ye may be tried; and ye shall have tribulation 10 days: be thou faithful unto death, and I will give thee a crown of life. **7:4** And I heard the number of them which were sealed: and there were sealed *144,000* of all the (*12*) tribes of the children of Israel. (KJV)

13. Who will have tribulation 10 days … … are the 144,000!

❖ **_The 144,000:_** *After being sealed and protected they will suffer tribulation!* ❖

They are "fed" 1,260 days!	144,000 are fed the Gospel! They will preach 30 days!	They will suffer 10 days tribulation!

2. How will the end be with a "flood"? (Page 1)

Serpent casts out "flood"!

Earth swallows the "flood":

Rev 9:2 And he (*fallen star/angel*) opened the bottomless pit; and there arose a smoke out of the pit, as the smoke of a great furnace. **3** And there came out of the smoke "*locusts*" upon the earth... **10** And they had tails like unto scorpions, and there were stings in their tails: and their power was to hurt men *5 months*.

Rev 12:15 And the *serpent* cast out of his mouth water as a "*flood*" after the woman... **16** And the earth helped the woman, and the earth opened her mouth, and swallowed up the "*flood*..." (KJV)

2. The end will be with … … a "flood" of (locusts) that return to the pit!

❖ *Flood: Locusts from the pit torment men 5 months & return to the earth!* ❖

---

11. When will armies surround Jerusalem? … (Pre) (Mid-week) (Post) … (Page 7)

Jerusalem surrounded!

Luke 21:20 When ye shall see Jerusalem compassed with armies, then know desolation is nigh...

Rev 16:12 (*6th Vial*) The great *River Euphrates*: and the water thereof was dried up, that the way of the kings of the east might be prepared. **16** And he gathered them into a place called in the Hebrew tongue Armageddon. **17** (*7th Vial*) And there came a great voice out of the temple of heaven, from the throne, saying, "It is done..." (KJV)

For I will gather all nations against Jerusalem to battle… Zech 14:2 (KJV)

11. Armies will surround Jerusalem … … (Post)

❖ *The Euphrates dries up & nations are gathered to Armageddon!* ❖

Serpent casts out "flood" | **Time of Trouble!** | **Jerusalem is surrounded!**
"Locusts" torment men 5 mos! | **Euphrates dries up!** | **Earth swallows "flood"**

---

12. When will the Abomination be set-up? … (Pre) (Mid-week) (Post) … (Page 8)

After 1,290 days:

Dan 9:27 And in the midst of the week (*7 years*) he shall cause the sacrifice and the oblation to cease… **12:11** And from the time that the daily sacrifice shall be taken away, and the abomination that makes desolate set up, there shall be *1,290 days*. (KJV)

12. The Abomination will be set-up … … (Post)

❖ *The Abomination will be set-up 1,290 days after sacrifice ends mid-week!* ❖

Mid-week: sacrifices end! | **1,290 days** | **Abomination is set-up!**

Archangel Michael defends Israel:

Dan 10:21 And there is none that holds with me (*Gabriel*) in these things, but *Michael* your prince. **12:1** At that time (*of trouble*) shall *Michael* stand up, the *great prince* which stands for the children of *thy people*... (KJV)

❖ *Israel fights battles (Dan 11) without Michael, the restrainer… II The 2:7* ❖

> **24.** **Where will Mystery, Babylon be found? (Page 21)**

Throne of Satan:

Rev 2:9 I know the blasphemy of those who say they are *Jews* and are not but are a *synagogue of Satan*...

Gen 49:16 *Dan* shall judge his people, as one of the tribes of Israel. **17** *Dan* shall be a serpent by the way, an adder in the path, that bites the horse's heels so that its rider shall fall backward.

Isa 22:21 And he (*anti-Christ*) shall be a father to the inhabitants of *Jerusalem*, and to the house of *Judah*.

Dan 11:37 Neither shall he regard the *God of his fathers* (*Jewish lineage*), nor the desire of women, nor regard any god: for he shall magnify himself above all.

> **24. Mystery, Babylon will be ... ... where Satan sets up his throne!**

"10 tribes" hate the Whore!

Rev 17:3 And I saw a woman sit upon a scarlet colored beast, full of names of blasphemy, having *"7 heads"* and 10 horns (*10 tribes*). **5** And upon her forehead was a name written MYSTERY, BABYLON THE GREAT, MOTHER OF HARLOTS AND ABOMINATIONS OF THE EARTH. **6** And I saw the woman drunken with the blood of the saints, and with the blood of the martyrs of Jesus. **16** And the *10 horns* which thou saw upon the beast, these shall hate the Whore (*Babylon*), and shall make her desolate and naked, and shall eat her flesh, and burn her with fire. (KJV)

7 Heads & 10 Horns (3 subdued):

Dan 7:8 I considered the horns and behold, there came up among them another *little horn* (*Anti-Christ*), before whom there were 3 (*kings*) of the first (*10*) horns plucked up by the roots. **23** The 4th beast shall be the 4th kingdom upon earth, which shall be diverse from all kingdoms, and shall devour the whole earth, and tread it down, and break it in pieces. **24** And the *10 horns* out of this kingdom are *10 kings* (*10 tribes*) that shall arise; and another (*Little horn*) shall rise after them; and he shall be diverse from the first, and he shall subdue *"3 kings"* (*3 tribes*).

❖ *7 Heads: anti-Christ shall subdue 3 of 10 kings/tribes! (Dan 7:24/Rev 17:3)* ❖

Israel flees "Babylon"!

Rev 18:2 And he cried mightily with a great voice, saying, Babylon the great is fallen, is fallen, and is become the habitation of devils…**4** I heard another voice from heaven, saying, "Come out of her My people, that ye be not partakers of her sins, and that ye receive not of her plagues. **5** Her sins have reached unto Heaven, and God hath remembered her iniquities." **10** Alas, alas, that great city Babylon, that mighty city! **24.** In her (*Jerusalem*) was found the blood of prophets and saints, and of all that were slain upon the earth. (KJV)

❖ *Anti-Christ rules the world with absolute power from Jerusalem!* ❖

Euphrates dries: 4 Angels are released!

Rev 9:15 And the 4 angels were loosed, which were prepared for *an hour*, a day, a month, and a year, for to slay the 3rd part of men. **16:12** The great river Euphrates; and the water thereof was dried up, that the way of the kings of the east might be prepared. **18:10** For in *one hour* is thy judgment come.

Rev 2:10 Fear none of those things which thou shalt suffer; and ye shall have tribulation *10 days*... (KJV)

❖ *One hour: Judgment that refers to the final 7 plagues!* ❖

7 heads & 10 horns /kings (3 subdued)!	**Mystery, Babylon!** Satan's throne: anti-Christ rules!	10 horns/tribes hate the Whore!

Northern Kingdom is dispersed!

Israel: 10 tribes disperse!

I Kings 11:31 And he said to (*king*) Jeroboam, "Take thee *10 pieces*"; for thus says the LORD, the God of Israel, "Behold, I will rend the kingdom out of the hand of Solomon, and will give *10 tribes* to thee…"

II Kings 17:6 In the 9th year of (*king*) Hoshea, the *king of Assyria* took Samaria (*10 tribes*) and carried *Israel* away into *Assyria*…

Hos 7:8 *Ephraim*, he hath mixed himself among the people; *Ephraim* is a cake not turned. **10:6** *Ephraim* shall receive shame, and *Israel* shall be ashamed of his own counsel… (KJV)

Sin of Jeroboam:

I Kings 12:31 He (*king Jeroboam*) made shrines on the high places, and made priests from every class of people, who were *not* of the sons *of Levi*. **29** And he set up *one* (*calf*) in *Bethel* (*House-of-God*), and the *other* he put, in *Dan*. **32** So he did at *Bethel*, sacrificing to the (*2*) *calves* that he had made. And at *Bethel* he installed the priests (*not of Levi*) of the high places which he had made. (KJV)

❖ **N. Kingdom**: *10 tribes of Israel (called Samaria, Ephraim or Dan) worship other gods!* ❖

Southern Kingdom remains!

Judah: 2 Tribes remain!

I Kings 12:21 And when (*King*) Rehoboam was come to *Jerusalem*, he assembled all the house of *Judah*, with the tribe of *Benjamin*… (KJV)

Northern Kingdom returns!

10 Tribes of Israel return:

Jer. 50:41 Behold, a people shall come from the *north*, and a *great nation* (*Israel*), and *many kings* (*10 tribes/ exiles*) shall be raised up from the coasts of the earth…

Ezekiel 37:21 And say unto them, Thus, says the Lord GOD; Behold, I will take the children (*exiles*) of *Israel* from among the heathen (*gentiles*), (*wherever*) they be gone, and will gather them on every side, and bring them into their own land… (KJV)

God is against/anti Gog!

King of the South returns:

Ezekiel 38:2 Son of man set your face *against* Gog (*Satan/anti-Christ*), of the land (*kingdom*) of *Magog* (*son of Japheth* **Gen 10:2**) **3** Thus says the Lord God: Behold, I am against you, O Gog (*Reuben's genealogy* **I Chr 5:4**), prince of *Rosh* (*Benjamin's son* **Gen 46:21**) and *Meshech & Tubal* (*Noah's grandsons* **I Chr 1:5**). **8** After many days thou shalt be visited (*remembered*): in the latter years thou (*10 tribes*) shalt come into the land (*Israel*) that is brought back from the sword (*dispersion*) and is gathered out of many people (*nations*), against the mountains of *Israel*, which have been always waste: but *it* (*Israel*) is brought forth out of the *nations*, and *they* shall dwell safely…

Genesis 49:16 *Dan* shall judge his people, as one of the tribes of Israel. **17** *Dan* shall be a serpent by the way…

Dan 11:28 Then shall he return into *his land* with great riches; and his heart shall be against the *Holy Covenant*; and he shall do exploits and return to his *own land* (*Israel*). **32** but the people that do *know their God* shall be strong and do exploits… (KJV)

❖ *First-Beast: called Little horn, anti-Christ; also, Gog, Dan, & king of the North!* ❖

These prophecies about the dispersed tribes of Israel began to be fulfilled in 1948!

Temple of the BRANCH!

Temple of the LORD!

Zech 6:12 Thus speaks the LORD of hosts, saying, Behold the man whose name is *"The BRANCH"*; and He shall grow up out of his place (*Heaven*), and He shall build the *Temple of the LORD*. **13** …and He shall bear the glory, and shall sit and rule upon His throne; and He shall be a priest… (KJV)

Know ye not that ye are the temple of God, & that the Spirit of God dwells in you? **I Cor 3:16** (KJV)

The "Wall" is cast down!

The Temple is raised up!

Eze 13:13 There shall be an overflowing shower in mine anger, and great hailstones in my fury to consume it. **14** So will I break down the *"wall"* that ye have daubed with *un-tempered mortar* and bring it down to the ground so that the foundation thereof shall be discovered, and it shall *fall*, and ye shall know that *I AM THE LORD*. **15** Thus will I accomplish my wrath upon the *"wall…"*
Amos 9:11 In that day will I raise up the *"tabernacle of David"* that is fallen and close-up the breaches thereof; and I will *raise-up* his ruins, and I will build it as in the days of old. (KJV)

❖ **The "wall" of "animal sacrifice" is <u>cast-down</u>; the temple of David is <u>raised-up</u>! ❖**

The "wall" is cast down!	Spiritual Temple!	Temple of David is raised!

❖ **Exiles build a physical temple, but Jesus builds a Spiritual temple! ❖**

The LORD on Mt. of Olives!

Second time for remnant!

Isa 11:11 And it shall come to pass in that day, that the Lord shall set his hand again the *"2nd time"* to recover the *"remnant"* of His people, which shall be left…
Zech 14:4 And His feet shall stand in that day upon the *Mount of Olives* which is before Jerusalem on the east, and the Mount of Olives shall cleave in the midst thereof toward the east and toward the west, and there shall be a very great valley; and half the mountain shall remove toward the north, and half of it toward the south. **7** But it shall be one day which shall be known to the LORD, not day, nor night: …at evening time it shall be light. (KJV)

JESUS is the LORD!

He no longer hides His face!

Eze 16:62 And I will establish My covenant with thee (*Israel*); and thou shalt know that *I am the LORD*. **39:29** Neither will I hide My face any more from them: for I have poured out My Spirit upon the house of Israel, says the Lord God.
Zech 14:9 And the Lord shall be King over all the earth. In that day shall there be one LORD, and His Name One.
Jer 31:31 The days come, says the LORD, that I will make a *"new covenant"* with Israel/Judah… (KJV)

He is Lord of lords, and King of kings; they that are with him are called, chosen, and faithful. **Rev 17:14** (KJV)

❖ **Israel is the object of the 7-year covenant and End-Time prophecy! ❖**

① 7-year Covenant: And he shall confirm the covenant with many for one week... Dan 9:27

One hour

2,300 days: then shall the sanctuary be cleansed! ~Dan 8:14 (KJV)

1,335 days: Blessed is he that waits! ~Dan 12:12 (KJV)

1,290 days: from end of Sacrifice to Abomination ~Dan 12:11

1,260 days: silence in heaven about half an hour! ~Rev 8:1

Half hour

For there is no answer from God ~Micah 3:7 (KJV)

1,260 days: woman (144,000) is nourished 3½ yrs. ~Rev 12:14

No one (else) could learn that song/Gospel ~Rev 14:3

1,260 days: Witness (Spirit of Elisha) prophesies! ~Rev 11:3

3½ years: to scatter power of the Holy people! ~Dan 12:7

3½ years: Little horn made war with the saints! ~Dan 7:21

42 mos: Power was given unto him/beast... Rev 13:5 (KJV)

Judgment: Persecution ~ Great Tribulation!

③ ...abominations shall be poured upon the desolate! ~ Dan 9:27

390 days shalt thou bear the iniquity of the house of Israel. ~Eze 4:5 (KJV)

30 days: The gospel shall be preached... then shall the end come. ~Mat 24:14 (KJV)

10 days: And ye (144,000) shall have tribulation... Rev 2:10 (KJV)

Falling away: Deception ~ Captivity ~ Doctrine of Balaam!

1,260 days: (Spirit of Elijah) prophesies! ~Rev 11:3

3½ years, 42 months, & 1,260 days: Although these lengths are the same and all the events occur during the 2nd half of the tribulation, they may not begin and end at the same time!

After 70 years: The LORD will visit Tyre/Jerusalem ~Isa 23:17 (KJV)
❖ 1948 - 2018 ❖

Knowing of His coming is such foolish wisdom, if we delay or die before we accept Jesus as Lord!

② Mid-week sacrifice ceases... Dan 9:27 (NKJ)

220 days | 1,000 days | 840 days | 420 days

30

40

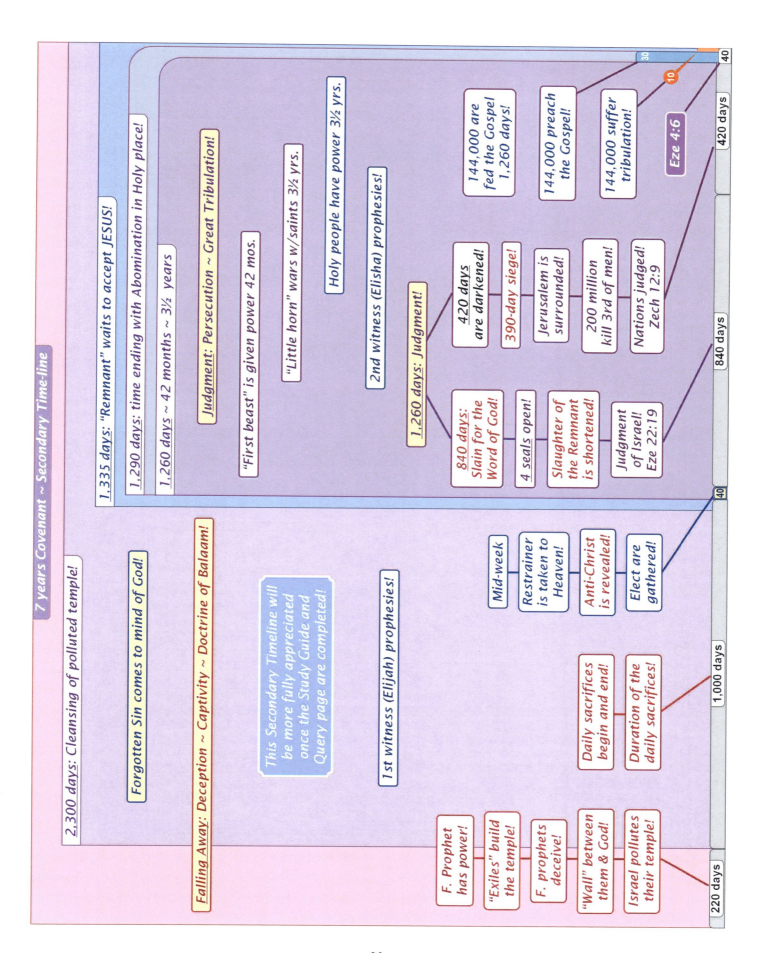

7 years Covenant ~ Secondary Time-line

2,300 days: Cleansing of polluted temple!

Forgotten Sin comes to mind of God!

Falling Away: Deception ~ Captivity ~ Doctrine of Balaam!

This Secondary Timeline will be more fully appreciated once the Study Guide and Query page are completed!

1st witness (Elijah) prophesies!

F. Prophet has power!

"Exiles" build the temple!

F. prophets deceive!

"Wall" between them & God!

Israel pollutes their temple!

Daily sacrifices begin and end!

Duration of the daily sacrifices!

Mid-week

Restrainer is taken to Heaven!

Anti-Christ is revealed!

Elect are gathered!

1,335 days: "Remnant" waits to accept JESUS!

1,290 days: time ending with Abomination in Holy place!

1,260 days ~ 42 months ~ 3½ years

Judgment: Persecution ~ Great Tribulation!

"First beast" is given power 42 mos.

"Little horn" wars w/saints 3½ yrs.

Holy people have power 3½ yrs.

2nd witness (Elisha) prophesies!

1,260 days: Judgment!

840 days: Slain for the Word of God!

4 seals open!

Slaughter of the Remnant is shortened!

Judgment of Israel! Eze 22:19

420 days are darkened!

390-day siege!

Jerusalem is surrounded!

200 million kill 3rd of men!

Nations judged! Zech 12:9

144,000 are fed the Gospel 1,260 days!

144,000 preach the Gospel!

144,000 suffer tribulation!

Eze 4:6

220 days | 1,000 days | 40 | 840 days | 420 days | 40 | 30 | 40

39

	Pre-rapture	Mid-tribulation	Post-rapture	
Page ix	**Deception!** he confirms covenant	**One-week Covenant ~ Dan 9:27** ...he ends sacrifice	**Judgment!** ...he makes desolate!	**Dan 9:27**
Page 1	The "wall" is built in troublesome times!	**Mid - week**	End is with a flood! (not flood of water)	**Dan 9:25**
Page 2	① Falling away comes first!	② "Restrainer" is taken! ③ "Wicked" is revealed! ④ Gathering together!	Day of Christ! ⑤ Day of the Lord!	**2 The 2:3-8**
Page 4	**Before His coming!** Tribulation those days! Not Gt. Tribulation! False prophets deceive!	**His coming!** Son of Man in power & glory! "Rapture" of Elect!	**Signs of the end!** Hated for Jesus' sake! Gospel is preached! Abomination is set-up!	**Page 5**
Page 10	**Israel's "captivity"** Peace: God calls no peace! "Sin" is remembered!		**Jacob's Trouble!** Jerusalem is surrounded: Nations are gathered!	**Page 11**
Page 14	**F. Prophet/beast as a lamb!** Speaks as a dragon! Power before 1st beast!	**Mid-week: Gathering together! (Rapture) Mat 24:31**	**Anti-Christ / First Beast** Beast: 7 heads & 10 horns! 1st beast: power 42 mos!	**Page 15**
Page 26	"Wall" is un-tempered! "Sin" altar profanes Jesus!		The "Wall" is cast down! BRANCH builds HIS Temple!	**Page 26**
Page 27	**Falling away!** Israel: backsliding heifer! Israel/Judah play Harlots!		**JESUS is a Sanctuary!** Stumbling Stone for Israel! "Israel/Zion" is engraved!	**Page 27**
Page 28	Un-tempered mortar! Israel's sin is un-covered!	Philadelphia is taken not tested!	Laodicea is tried in fire! Animal blood uncovers sin!	**Pages 29/30**
Page 29	Michael restrains iniquity of Satan ~ 2 The 2:7	(Michael) is taken! (Beast) is revealed!	42 mos: time of gentiles! Little horn in Jerusalem!	**Pages 30/31**
Page 35	7 heads & 10 horns /kings (3 subdued)!	**Mystery, Babylon!** Satan's throne: beast rules!	10 horns/tribes hate the Whore!	**Dan 7:24 Rev 17:3**
Pages 26/28	Un-tempered "wall"! "Altar of blood sacrifice"	Spiritual Temple: Jesus' blood covers sin!	"Wall" is cast-down! David's temple is raised!	**Page 37**

Three columns display prophetic events before and after a "Mid-week" Rapture!